the **Rolling Stones** files

the Rolling Stones files

Exclusive! 400 recently discovered photographs
from the Daily Mirror archive!

Mark Paytress

Foreword by Chris Jagger

CLB

5144 The Rolling Stones Files

Produced by Quadrillion Publishing Ltd in association with Bookman Projects Ltd.

This edition published in1999 by CLB International, an imprint of Quadrillion Publishing Ltd, Godalming Business Centre, Woolsack Way, Godalming, Surrey GU7 1XW, England.

Distributed in the U.S. by Quadrillion Publishing Inc., 230 Fifth Avenue, NY, NY 10001

credits

Commissioning Editor: Will Steeds
Project Editor: Suzanne Evins
Design: Justina Leitão
Americanizer: Beverly LeBlanc
Picture Research: Hugh Gallacher; Mark Paytress
Production: Neil Randles

For Bookman Projects Ltd: Nick Kent; Hugh Gallacher

Printed and bound in Singapore
ISBN 1-84100-261-5

prelim and end pictures

Half-title page: Screaming at the Stones, Nelson, Lancashire, England, 1964.

Title page: Empty glasses, full itinerary!

Page 4: December 15, 1967: A pile of records, including a Four Tops single called, appropriately, "I Keep Running Away," on the back seat of Brian Jones' Rolls-Royce.

Page 6: Chris Jagger leaves court, December 1967.

Page 7: April 1964: The Stones amid a sea of lights at the Empire Pool, Wembley, London.

Page 159: July 25, 1964: Stewards attend to the damage after riots at the Imperial Ballroom, Nelson.

Page 160: Photo call at London's Green Park, January 11, 1967.

a note on currency values

Most currencies in the text are stated in pounds sterling, at their contemporary value. The approximate contemporary U.S. dollar equivalent was $2.80 = £1 from 1963 to 1967; and $2.40 = £1 from November 1967 to 1974.

contents

foreword

IF YOU CAN'T REMEMBER the 1960s then you haven't read your own press-cuttings, as the saying goes. Here is an opportunity to catch up. Leaving a restaurant, picking up a phone, or entering a courtroom, a photographer would be lurking to snap a Rolling Stone and record the moment for posterity. Occasionally, I might be in the background, melting into the shadows somewhere!

Off-guard pictures can reveal so much more than posed ones, as every photographer knows. Nobody wants the official record company's studied portrait, but would prefer the artist slurping cornflakes in an old bathrobe with the corny caption of "Snap, Crackle & Pop." The early period of this book probably marks the first dawnings of what we now know today as the paparazzi.

I have seen both sides of the story. Permission to take photos around well-known bands has become so tight recently that anyone with an instamatic camera is suspected of planning secret licensing deals to manufacture T-shirts and coffee mugs. A few years ago I wrote a review of Eric Clapton at London's Albert Hall for a music paper and rang his office for a photo. Surprisingly, Roger Forrester, Eric's manager, answered the call and said maybe there was a picture in a drawer someplace, and I duly received the same snap as appeared on his latest record cover, a regal picture of Sir Eric posing in an Armani suit. This was hardly a scoop, so, instead, I contacted a paparazzo I knew who happened to be at the show unofficially and had taken a couple of nice pictures before he was thrown out of the gig.

On the other hand, photographers who came to Ian Stewart's ("the sixth Rolling Stone") funeral were fortunate not to have their cameras wrapped around their necks and film pushed into their mouths for the intrusion into a very moving occasion.

The majority of the pictures here were by invitation, and looking back to those early days there is a charming innocence in the snaps of the band trying on jackets in a Hollywood store. The action pictures of Brian and Keith playing soccer on the beach at Malibu could be from anyone's vacation album. (But why is Keith wearing

a "Chadwick School" sweatshirt?) If Joe Bloggs has a minor prang in his car it's hard to attract a policeman today (even my insurance company lack interest), but Mick appears to have his own photographer in tow to immortalize the moment when the Countess of Argyll "in her Ford Anglia" ran into that tank of an Aston Martin DB6. Unsurprisingly, like anyone in that position, Mick looks furious announcing "it's going to cost me £200."

Where do you draw the line on intrusive pictures though? Pressmen peering through

the windows of Keith's house at Redlands where the *News of the World* organized that infamous drug bust? There was a spontaneous demonstration outside the paper's offices in Fleet Street after that disgraceful episode, which sent Robert Fraser to prison and involved a connivance far worse than experimenting with dope in the privacy of your own home.

Leafing through these photos you sometimes wish for color. The jackets in striped green velvet, the purple hats, and bright shirts would all tell of a time when a fashion statement was more than wearing a blue Adidas top and white sneakers. Perhaps some coloring pens could be provided? Exactly what was Mick wearing as he sat next to a very prim, and rather slim, Mrs Mary Whitehouse with her legs glued together? Some listed details give away the importance of the situation. We are told that the late arrival of Mr. Harrison "had delayed the train's departure, the 15:05 from Euston," and that Andrew Oldham had bumped into a couple of Beatles in Mayfair (as you do) and asked them for a song for the Stones, a request which was naturally granted.

There are the quotes, supplied over a period of thirty years and frequently wittier than your average politician; no wonder the words of rock stars were sought on every subject. With any luck the quotes would be spontaneous or outrageous or both, and then they would have to spend the next six months living them down.

One thing missing in a book, naturally, is the music. Pictures tell a story, but the story of this band was really told in sound rather than light, so that's worth bearing in mind as you read through—that's what was important to these guys and their fans. Perhaps rifle through your collection for a scratched copy of "Five by Five" as you turn the pages of *The Rolling Stones Files*, not just a fan's book, but a seminal record of the scene in the 1960s.

introduction

THE OPPORTUNITY TO WALTZ INTO one of the world's finest photographic archives and sift through thousands of crumbling 10 x 8 prints, contact sheets and, best of all, rest a spyglass on strips of well-preserved, but hitherto unprocessed, negatives, was irresistible. There have, of course, been countless books on the Rolling Stones, and I have most of them. But it took just one inspection of that particular collection, which belongs to the *Daily Mirror,* a leading British daily newspaper, to persuade me that there was more than enough material to create a unique pictorial chronicle of the Rolling Stones.

What you'll see in *The Rolling Stones Files* are more than 400 of the best photographs from that huge reservoir of images. Many, developed from negatives for the first time, are previously unseen. Quite a few have rarely been sighted since their first publication, either in the *Daily Mirror* or in one of its sister newspapers or magazines. Those that might be familiar hail from photo sessions deemed too good, or too historically significant, to ignore.

One additional decision had to be made. The Rolling Stones' career is soon to extend into its fifth decade. Should we attempt to chronicle it in full, or restrict ourselves to a specific era? Two factors helped force our hand. With one or two notable exceptions, there was little in the *Daily Mirror* archive after the mid-seventies that couldn't be found in any other respected photo library. And while the Rolling

Stones have become an institution without tarnishing too much of their reputation, it is the decade between 1964 and 1974, on which that reputation inevitably rests.

It was during the sixties that the pop industry as we know it was invented. And that was thanks, in a large part, to the Beatles. They inspired acres of newsprint, thousands of pieces of memorabilia and sold millions of records to a huge global audience. Inevitably, the Beatles were every news reporter's favorite pop group. Just as their music sold records in quantities hitherto unimaginable, their all-smiling, family-friendly faces sold newspapers.

But just as light needs dark, and sin requires a sanctuary, another voice from the emergent youth culture was required. That "voice," the abrasive sight and sounds of the Rolling Stones, was altogether more difficult to assimilate into the mainstream. The headlines the Stones produced weren't simply celebrations of Britishness, success, and the easy alliance of the generations. In many ways, they told the true story of the sixties, the one which suggested necessary shifts in class, morality, and taste were not going to be secured without a struggle. From the outset, the Rolling Stones signified liberation and revolt, and various scandals, many involving matters of sex and drugs, dogged their career.

Unlike the Beatles, the Stones rarely got involved in prearranged photo sessions where they'd be expected to conform to a photographer's visual pun. That's not to say

there aren't several revealing exclusives in the book. During the early months of the Stones' success, *Daily Mirror* photographers caught them in various uncharacteristic poses. Two sessions, shot on the Stones' first American trip, are a testament to the thrill of making it to their musical spiritual home. Three years later, and in the midst of various drug busts, the band invited another *Mirror* photographer to capture them at work in a recording studio.

A word, too, about the *Daily Mirror.* Unarguably, the newspaper of sixties Britain, the *Mirror* showed far more enthusiasm for pop than its conservative rivals. Their reporters, Patrick Doncaster ("the *Mirror*'s DJ"), and later Don Short, gamely sought to keep up with the trends, but even they sometimes reported on young musicians as if they'd just dropped out of the sky. But where other newspapers would only heap abuse, the *Mirror* at least documented, and occasionally sought to understand the new phenomenon, a stand that was most marked in the paper's even-handed attitude to the decline of Brian Jones. And what other newspaper could invite itself into Mick Jagger's home—and with a trio of fans in tow? Those *were* different times.

the photographers

THE *DAILY MIRROR* EMPLOYED a staff of around two dozen photographers during the sixties, all of whom were expected to cover a variety of assignments. "The picture editor at that time preferred us to cover a wide range of topics so we'd not become stale," recalls Doreen Spooner, for many years the only woman in the team. Consequently, shooting the Rolling Stones —at a pop concert, in a recording studio, outside court, or in an airport lounge— was a job that might have landed in the lap of any of the team irrespective of their interest in pop. Instead, the unifying ethos was professionalism.

Among the staffers and stringers who helped document the Rolling Stones' first decade, and whose work is represented in this book are: Tom Buist, David Cole, Vic Crawshaw, Freddie Crewett, Kent Gavin, Eric Harlow, Michael Irwin, Tom King, Charles Ley, Alisdair MacDonald, Cyril Maitland, Stan May, Arthur Murray, Charles Owens, Eric Piper, Tony Sellers, Arthur Sidney, Doreen Spooner, Dennis Stone, and Peter Stone.

"There was nothing bland about the Rolling Stones," remembers Peter Stone, one of the group's more regular observers. "They were so unusual and everything they did was outrageous. They were true rock 'n' rollers." But, according to Stone and colleagues such as Vic Crawshaw, who shot the group many times as they passed through London (later Heathrow) Airport, the *Daily Mirror* photographers were rarely exposed to the band's "bad-boy" side. "Back in the sixties," Vic recalls, "all the pop stars wanted to have their photographs taken. They were pleased to see you, they'd stop and pose, they'd do what you wanted. It was all very gentlemanly and polite. After all, they were after the publicity." Kent Gavin, now the *Daily Mirror*'s Chief Photographer, concurs: "The groups weren't distrustful in those days. It was only when the Sunday papers started digging into their private lives that things changed."

The Rolling Stones, who, at the instigation of manager Andrew Oldham, were happy to set themselves up as a disruptive element in opposition to the Beatles' apparent homeliness, had good reason to distrust the prying lenses of the press photographers. As court regulars, incriminating shots could have been used against them. The *Daily Mirror*, as the most popular newspaper in Britain, had more influence than most, but the generally encouraging tone it took to pop music made it virtually the pop star's friend. "In those days the *Mirror* was the biggest and the best, and we enjoyed a good relationship with the bands," insists Peter Stone. "Jagger liked the *Mirror*, and Les Perrin, their PR guy, was an ex-*Mirror* man, I think, too."

While Vic Crawshaw makes no claim to being a pop fan, and "shouldn't think that Mick Jagger would remember me," Stone was a rock 'n' roll enthusiast from Windsor and a contemporary of the new pop groups. He first shot the Rolling Stones at a press call in London's Green Park in 1967, and after covering them in the recording studio, in concert, and at landmark events such as the *Beggars Banquet* album launch and the *Rolling Stones Rock 'n' Roll Circus*, he was able to claim a degree of intimacy with the band, and with head honcho Mick Jagger in particular.

"There was this massive reception for Mick after a gig in Paris," Stone remembers. "Two or three hundred French people were waiting for this superstar to walk in.

above 30 June 1967: "Your verdict, Mr. Jagger?" Mick's car is besieged by reporters after leaving court in Chichester, Sussex.

I, as a good old journo, had done my job and was at the bar having a beer. As he walked in, all these smart Parisian heads turned toward him. He surveyed the scene, came straight across and said, 'For Chrissake, Stoney, get me a beer!' That's how it was in those days."

Kent Gavin, too, became a regular face on the Stones' travels: "I went round the U.S. with them in 1975," he recalls, "and I wanted to take shots of them on the site of the Alamo where many Englishmen died in battle. Mick thought it was a great idea. Ten days passed and I couldn't get them out of bed. Time was running out—I had a pressing assignment with Bing [Crosby] and

"There was nothing bland about the Rolling Stones."

Peter Stone

Frank [Sinatra]. Mick saved me. He made them drive past the site and then kicked 'em all out of the car! The band thought they were going to the airport."

Both Kent Gavin and Peter Stone maintain that it was Jagger who took most interest in the photographers and the publicity side of the band's affairs. "Mick was always interested in the camera," says Gavin. "He was an actor, after all." But, he adds, that didn't always translate with some of the writers. "Mick avoided some of them like the plague. But he did build up a good relationship with the *Daily Mirror* and with our pop writer Don Short. I'm glad to say that we had a good relationship with both the Stones and the Beatles."

Doreen Spooner reckons pop music was "the tabloid's dream, especially because there were always pretty girls involved." "Fans became the news story," says Crawshaw. That may have been so in the early days, but when the public tired of seeing shots of screaming girls at pop concerts, their appetite for the new pop heroes had not dimmed. As the antidote to the Beatles, the Rolling Stones continued to make the headlines. "Some of that 'bad-boy' image couldn't have been manufactured— obviously they wouldn't have wanted to get busted for drugs," says Peter Stone. "But at the same time, you had the Beatles wearing their trimmed haircuts, their trimmed suits with little black ties and neat little collars,

right Part of the team of *Daily Mirror* photographers who shot the Stones during the sixties (from the top): Vic Crawshaw, Doreen Spooner, Kent Gavin, and Peter Stone.

and here you've got Keith Richard looking as though he's just fallen out of a bar in Bangkok!" Although Vic Crawshaw remembers the band being less cooperative than the Beatles, according to Stone, "the Rolling Stones were not control freaks. They weren't bad boys in our eyes either. That came from the style of music and the concerts."

All are agreed that the glory days of star photography have long since passed; that the spontaneous, candid, and unauthorized photojournalism you see in this book would not be possible today. "In the sixties, there were none of those massive photo calls that you get now, where everyone basically gets the same picture," insists Doreen Spooner. "We'd have been fired if we came back with something like that!" Kent Gavin agrees: "Pop pictures are not something I'd like to do now. Look at the control a group like the Spice Girls have. They give photographers two minutes on stage. They make sure the lighting is bad, and they avoid standing together for a group shot. Then they make you sign a declaration that the photos are only to be used for one purpose only." Peter Stone explains: "This was all prepaparazzi days when photographers could be trusted. In fact, there was a mutual trust—that way, you'd get the shots you wanted, and they'd get the publicity they wanted."

The development of the long-focus lens alienated the stars from their pictorial chroniclers for obvious intrusive reasons. And, according to Stone, it has also reduced the intimacy of the photographer/star situation. "When we shot the Stones at Green Park, for example, we worked within yards, or even feet, of the group because of the nature of the equipment. There was none of this keeping the press on one side of the street behind barriers." He claims that Harold Wilson, the British "pop" prime minister, was the first to keep photographers at bay.

Stone was one of the few photographers afforded the privilege of shooting the group while they worked in a recording studio. "That was an all-night session down at the Olympic Studios in Barnes when Brian Jones was around," he remembers. "He was dressed in a frilly, curtain-type lacy number and noshing at a carry-out meal. They were unusual, they were unique, and to actually get near to them, in retrospect, is a remarkable situation. But at the time I really didn't think much of it."

Chapter One 1964
READY, STEADY, GO!

OFFERED TO THE PUBLIC as an antidote to those all-singing, all-smiling, all-round entertainers the Beatles, the Rolling Stones endured the wrath of the adult world for much of their early career. In one of the first notable stories on the group, published on May 29, 1964, the *Daily Mirror* chose not to mince its words: "They are the ugliest group in Britain. They are not looked upon very kindly by most parents or adults in general ... "

These bad boys from the suburbs of London drew their musical inspiration from the bluesmen of black America, and their robust, antisocial attitude from fifties' rock 'n' roll. Having built up an enthusiastic fan base in the capital's R&B clubs, the Stones secured a record deal in May 1963, and took off on their first national tour in September, supporting their R&B idol Bo Diddley. By the start of 1964, they were being tipped as the Beatles' closest rivals.

The Rolling Stones capitalized on the success of their early records—"Come On," "I Wanna Be Your Man," "Not Fade Away," "It's All Over Now"—with a grueling concert schedule. This chapter chronicles the frenzied nature of those early performances. On stage, the band (particularly Mick Jagger and Brian Jones) shake their maracas and tambourines, their hips, and their hair, in a manner rarely seen before on a British or American stage. In the audience, teenage girls wave placards and posters. And screeeeam! Their elder brothers occasionally show their appreciation in more destructive ways.

As long-forgotten stories unfold in the text, candid photographs visibly illustrate the Stones' growing confidence, their surly expressions peering out beneath increasingly unruly hair. Already, they are making occasional visits to court. But there is a great sense of fun, too—witness the frolics in a boutique during an early visit to the United States, the home of the music that inspired them. ■

> "They are the ugliest group in Britain. They are not looked upon very kindly by parents or adults ..."
> *Daily Mirror*

left The band relaxing on Malibu Beach, Los Angeles, on June 4, 1964, during a break on their first, and not particularly successful, American tour.

1964

In April 1964, Mr. Wallace Scowcroft, President of the National Federation of Hairdressers, offers a free haircut to the next chart-topping pop act. "The Rolling Stones are the worst," he adds.

The Stones are ridiculed on American TV in June 1964 by Dean Martin. After a trampoline act finishes, he tells the audience: "That's the Rolling Stones' father. He's been trying to kill himself ever since."

The Stones interrupt their U.S. tour to honor an engagement at the Magdalen College Commemoration Ball, in Oxford, England. Although the fee was just £100, and the air fares £1,500, the Stones are obliged to fulfil the obligation: "Sorry, but that's the fee you signed for a year ago," they are told, "and we can't increase it a penny more."

A storm erupts after the group's "charmless" appearance on BBC-TV's *Juke Box Jury* in July 1964. Their crime? Smoking throughout the program, and making negative comments about every record played on the show.

The group's publicists upped the controversy for the Stones' fall 1964 U.S. tour. A press statement reads: "The Rolling Stones, who haven't bathed in a week, arrived here for their second U.S. tour yesterday!"

The band fail to turn up to record a session for BBC Radio in November, prompting reports of a six-month ban. According to Mick Jagger, they knew nothing about the bookings. "They were made on our behalf, but we never consented to them," he says. The Stones patch it up with "the Beeb" and are back in the Corporation's studios by spring 1965.

The Stones might have looked and sounded unruly, but contrary to popular opinion, they weren't dirty. Brian Jones was so obsessed about his hair, sometimes washing it twice a day, that the band called him Mr. Shampoo.

At the end of the year, Oldham places a seasonal message on behalf of the Stones in national magazines: "Happy Christmas to the starving hairdressers and their families ... "

the Beatles' latest rivals

above Manager Andrew Oldham advised the band to wear Beatles-inspired uniforms for television shows or special concerts, such as the Great Pop Prom. But those ironed shirts and attractive leather vests didn't last long.

right September 15, 1963: An orderly crowd gathers at the stage door of the Royal Albert Hall, London, after the Great Pop Prom. The Beatles topped the bill; newcomers the Rolling Stones were there to make up the numbers.

IN 1964, NO ONE KNEW whether the beat boom bubble was about to burst, or if it would roll on for a few more months before fizzling out—just like rock 'n' roll and skiffle had done in the late fifties. That uncertainty helps explain the punishing workload undertaken by the Rolling Stones during their first full year as professional musicians: They toured Britain four times and hit the United States twice before the end of 1964.

The band had been working the clubs continually since January 1963, when drummer Charlie Watts joined Mick Jagger (vocals, harmonica), Keith Richard (guitar), Brian Jones (guitar, harmonica), and Bill Wyman (bass). The Stones played three or four nights a week in and around London, before they signed with Decca Records and released their debut single, "Come On," in June. With support from their record company, sympathetic pop papers like the *Record Mirror*,

and the enterprising talents of their new manager Andrew Oldham, the Stones' profile was upped considerably during the fall of 1963.

On September 15, the band propped up the bill at the Great Pop Prom, one of those great beat-era extravaganzas, which took place at the Royal Albert Hall, in London. Playing to their biggest audience yet, the Stones were not overawed, and duly secured a rapturous response from the young crowd. However, they did made one notable concession, by exchanging their scruffy club clothes for a neat, Beatles-like uniform complete with leather vests. The Great Pop Prom was the first of only two occasions where the Stones played on the same bill as the Beatles, who inevitably headlined both shows.

Although later posited as rivals by the popular press (with a little prompting from Andrew Oldham), the relationship between the Beatles and the Stones was more than amicable. When the Stones were struggling in the London clubs and still without a record deal, the Beatles came along to offer encouragement, most notably one evening in April 1963 at the Crawdaddy Club, in suburban Richmond. After the show, the two groups adjourned to the Stones' dingy

"Now the Beatles have registered with all age groups, the Rolling Stones have taken over as the voice of the teens."

Daily Express

flat in Edith Grove, Chelsea, where the Beatles invited the London R&B combo to see them perform at the Top Pop Proms at the Royal Albert Hall a few days later. Jagger, Richard, and Jones attended, and in a much-reported moment, Brian Jones was mobbed (mistakenly) after the show as he helped carry the Beatles' equipment out. It was an experience he didn't forget.

On September 10, just days before the Great Pop Prom, Andrew Oldham bumped into John Lennon and Paul McCartney in Mayfair and explained that the Stones were having difficulty in finding the right song for their second single. The three drove to the recording studio where the Stones were working, and by the end of the evening, the Beatles' songwriters had fixed the problem by offering them a new song, "I Wanna Be Your Man."

In later years, Lennon often complained that whatever the Beatles did, the Stones would do a couple of months later, but at this stage in their careers, John and Paul were eager for as many acts to record their songs as possible.

A second national tour at the start of 1964 helped the Stones' third single, a Bo Diddley-inspired cover of Buddy Holly's "Not Fade Away," into the British Top Three, confirming the promise they'd shown the previous year. The band shared the spotlight with visiting American all-girl trio the Ronettes, although it soon became clear which act proved to be the real headliners.

right (left to right) Mick Jagger, Keith Richard, Brian Jones, Bill Wyman, and Charlie Watts. The Stones pose by their tour bus with their guitars and trademark unsmiling expressions. It's early January 1964 and the group have just begun their second British tour.

far right The Rolling Stones rarely posed for portraits, and when they did, they shunned the "cheeky chappie" demeanor of John, Paul, George, and Ringo in favor of a look that suggested—at least in January 1964—confrontation. "Their success seems to lie in their off-handedness," opined the *Daily Sketch*.

MODS!

IT'S APRIL 9, 1964, and the two topics that would dominate the British press for that year—the General Election and the rivalry between two aggressive youth cults, "Mods" and "Rockers"—jostled for prominence on the front pages.

An early flashpoint came at the Mad Mod Ball, organized by the Variety Club of Great Britain in conjunction with the makers of TV's *Ready, Steady, Go!* pop show. Inside the Empire Pool, Wembley, over 8,000 pop fans raised the roof as they

welcomed a succession of top groups. It was a different story outside the venue, where a menacing crowd of "Rockers" had gathered for a confrontation with the departing audience at the end of the show.

The arrival of police reinforcements thwarted the impending showdown—but not without first making more than thirty arrests. "They are likely to be charged with insulting behavior or causing an obstruc- tion," a police spokesman explained. The "Rockers" had congregated in the road out- side the hall after the Ball had begun and additional police officers were called when the troublemakers began riding up and down the forecourt of the Empire Pool on their motorbikes. "With headlights blazing, they drove between police and pedestrians, shouting and revving their engines," report- ed the *Daily Mirror*, before the police took control and sealed off the forecourt.

Inside, the mood was less threatening but no less peaceable. Despite having just enjoyed their first real success with "Not Fade Away," the Rolling Stones were by no means the biggest stars on a bill that also included Cilla Black, Billy J. Kramer and the Dakotas, the Searchers, the Fourmost,

the Merseybeats, Freddie and the Dreamers, Sounds Incorporated, Kenny Lynch, Kathy Kirby, and Manfred Mann. But having whipped the crowd into a frenzy with their short, dynamic—though mimed—set, it was they who stole the headlines by almost

"They are likely to be charged with insulting behavior or causing an obstruction."

police spokesman

causing a riot inside the venue. As they tried to leave the revolving rostrum, the group were mobbed. It was 30 minutes before the Rolling Stones reached the relative safety of the backstage area.

Not everyone enjoyed the show, which had also been televised. The *Daily Mirror*'s Richard Sear wrote: "The singers were hopeless. [They] mimed to their records and that meant that their words came from an entirely different place to where they were standing." And the audience? Dressed "in a variety of garbs and expressions," sniffed Sear.

facing page April 8, 1964: The Stones pictured during a break in rehearsal for the Mad Mod Ball show at the Empire Pool, Wembley, in suburban London.

above and below left No escape. The movable podium placed in the middle of the venue was intended to give the audi- ence a better view. But it caused problems when the band attempted to leave the stage.

inset Handbags, glad rags and autograph books—all vital accoutrements of the Modish pop fan, circa April '64. This horde of enthusiasts was hoping for a glimpse of the stars before making its way into the Mad Mod Ball.

BY SPRING 1964, the Beatles were entitled to look over their shoulders. The Rolling Stones had little hope of eclipsing the Fab Four at the 12th *New Musical Express* Poll Winners' All-Star Concert on April 26. (The show was subsequently televised as *Big Beat '64*.) But the release of the Stones' debut album, which went straight to No. 1, bringing to an end the Beatles' 11-month unbroken run at the top, had shaken up the Merseysiders.

big beat '64

The Poll Winners' show brought the Stones back to the Empire Pool, Wembley, for the second time in a month. While they weren't up for any prizes yet, they did, according to the *NME*'s Graeme Andrews, win the second biggest reception of the day: "With Mick on maracas and Brian on harmonica, the way-out five could hardly be heard above the shouts … I was sitting two rows from the rostrum and I couldn't hear any of it through the screams."

Such was British teenagers' passion for pop that the 20,000 fans who'd crammed in to the two shows (afternoon and evening) were blissfully unconcerned that a similar bill had been assembled for the Mad Mod Ball—with one notable exception, the Beatles. This time, "Beatlemania!" was back in its "screaming, shaking, twisting" glory, reported the *Daily Mirror*. Indeed, the newspaper chose to ignore the Rolling Stones completely, while happily reporting the presence of a "galaxy of stars," among them Cliff Richard and the Shadows, the Hollies, Joe Brown, the Dave Clark Five,

facing page Mick Jagger's slacks-and-sweater attire was felt worthy of comment in reports of the show. But the main bone of contention was the band's hair, which had earlier prompted the *Daily Sketch* to write that the Stones' appearance was "straight out of the Stone Age."

top and below far left From intense to ecstatic, the Rolling Stones live experience provoked some extreme reactions from the fans. The *Big Beat '64* banner behind the audience advertises a forthcoming TV broadcast of the show.

below left May 3, 1964: Backstage at the Palace Theatre, Manchester, with a selection of gifts thrown on stage by adoring fans. As the years rolled on, the gifts were often of a more intimate persuasion.

the Swinging Blue Jeans, Brian Poole and the Tremeloes, Big Dee Irwin, and Gerry and the Pacemakers (who lined up alongside many of the previously mentioned Mod Ball participants).

It was inevitable that the Beatles' first British show in several months would grab the headlines, but backstage, they congratulated the Stones (in some ways still their protégés) on their performance, both on stage and on their new LP. Not everyone was so enamored of the album. "Their singles have a strange appeal, but the LP is a stinker," wrote Mike Nevard in the *Daily Herald*. Not that the Stones seemed to mind any negative publicity. Indeed, by this time, they'd begun to thrive on it.

A report on their recent runaway success in the *Daily Mirror* on April 29, clearly understood that a degree of contrariness was central to the band's appeal: "They are even used to the type of article that asks big brother if he would let his sister go out with one of them. But an awful lot of people

love 'em—those five shaggy-as-Shetland-ponies lads known as the Rolling Stones. One hundred and ten thousand people in Britain forked out nearly £200,000 across the record counters for their first LP—simply titled *The Rolling Stones*." Asked for his comments, Jagger happily twisted the knife: "I never did like wearing a suit," he said. "Maybe I'll like a suit when I'm 25."

To add to the Stones' most successful month yet, the band made their first venture overseas on April 19, flying in to Switzerland to film a *Ready, Steady, Go!* special in Montreux. When they took off for their third British tour at the start of May, they virtually guaranteed a stack of summer headlines—and the continuing success of their first LP.

Meanwhile, debate over the validity of the Stones' music, and also their worth as human beings, was waged in both the popular and the music press. In May, this culminated in a "For" and "Against" cover story featured in the pages of *Melody Maker*.

Promised land

ON JUNE 1, and with their self-titled debut album riding high on the British chart, the Rolling Stones boarded a plane at London Airport bound for the United States, then in the grip of Beatlemania. Although a crowd of 500 fans were waiting at Kennedy Airport, New York, to greet them, there was not a subsequent Stones chart invasion. Sometimes, especially when they strayed from the east and west coasts and into the American heartlands, the group found themselves performing to half-empty halls. But wherever they went, they made news. After all, they were English, they wore their hair long, and they were best friends with the ever-popular Beatles.

The Rolling Stones' first American visit was a pilgrimage as much as anything else, which was why they arranged a visit to the Chess recording studios in Chicago, after they hit the city on June 9. Chess was the home of R&B, the place where the Stones' idols like Chuck Berry, Muddy Waters, and Willie Dixon had been recording their songs for years. The band spent a couple of days there, too, hoping some of the studio's magic might rub off on their own work.

It did. "It's All Over Now" gave the Stones their first British No. 1 single, and the blues-heavy "Five By Five" EP enhanced the band's reputation as R&B purists with a mission to propagate the cause. By the end of the year, "Little Red Rooster," perhaps one of the most uncommercial songs ever to top the British singles' chart, marked the peak of the Stones' R&B achievements. From this moment on, it was the songwriting team of Mick Jagger and Keith Richard that dictated the group's inexorable progress to become, by 1970, the self-styled "greatest rock 'n' roll band in the world."

"They're outrageous! They're rebels. They sell! They're England's hottest—but hottest —group."

London Records' advert in *Billboard*

facing page After landing in New York, the Stones gave two press conferences, the first in an airport lounge. Later, they entertained the press a second time from the Astor Hotel, where they patiently answered a lot of silly questions about their hair. Even the usually reticent Charlie Watts was moved to address the audience. Outside, reported the *Daily Mirror*, "teenage girls armed with scissors" had apparently caught a "curl for a souvenir" fever.

above Mick Jagger soon emerged as the group's chief spokesman. By the end of the tour, he was telling reporters: "I give the Rolling Stones about another two years." The Stateside edition of their debut album was subtitled "England's Newest Hitmakers" in a bid to capitalize on the Beatles-inspired "British Invasion".

below Charlie Watts, always perceived as the most gentlemanly Stone, obliges an American convert.

above Get the feeling Charlie Watts wishes he was somewhere else?

Stones on the beach

"They are quite different from the Beatles, and more terrifying. The effect is sex ... "

Vogue

From New York, the group took a five-hour flight to Los Angeles where, on June 4, they posed for this unlikely photo session on Malibu Beach. According to the photographer's report, "The boys had some hamburgers, played some ball, and were just happy to be out by the water." Apparently, it was too cold to go swimming.

While in Los Angeles preparing for their live American debut in San Bernadino, the Stones went on a shopping spree at Beau Gentry on Vine Street, Hollywood, where they spent about $500 on clothes.

fab gear bonanza

"The Rolling Stones dress very clean and smart when they relax, contrary to what people might think."

Jimmy Savile, *The People*

ALTHOUGH THE STONES' first American visit was only moderately successful, it was a different story at home, where their album had spent three months at No. 1 and expectations were high for their long-awaited follow-up single to "Not Fade Away." After a short vacation, the band returned to their seemingly endless tour of the provinces, where their increasingly familiar repertoire was greeted by ecstatic, sometimes riotous scenes. When, on July 8, a report on the Beatles' party after the premiere of their film, *A Hard Day's Night*, was headlined "The Night Three Stones Rolled In," clearly things had changed.

Even the Stones' girlfriends had become news. Most prominent was Mick's relationship with Christine "Chrissie" Shrimpton. Theirs was the first of the great Swinging London romances—pop upstart dates sister of top model Jean "The Shrimp" Shrimpton—but in the light of Jagger's subsequent liaisons, it was covered with some dignity by the press. The view from the inside was quite different: The pair argued almost continuously throughout their relationship, and it's believed that Shrimpton inspired some of Jagger's most vitriolic lyric put-downs in songs such as "Under My Thumb" and "Back Street Girl." By the time Chrissie had a job at Radio Caroline where, according to the *Daily Mirror*, she was "the girl who answers the pirate station's fan mail," she'd been Jagger's live-in partner for almost a year.

When it was announced on July 6, 1964 that the Stones' latest single, "It's All Over Now," had topped the charts, Chrissie Shrimpton was vacationing with Mick in Ibiza, quaintly described in the press as "a Mediterranean island off Spain." With the rest of the band similarly out of sight, it was left to Brian Jones to come out to play for the photographers. Replacing the Animals' "The House Of The Rising Sun," the Stones' latest success was another cover version, this time of a hit by the Valentinos.

left Chrissie Shrimpton, sister of top model Jean, was the first in a distinguished line of Rolling Stones celebrity girlfriends. By June 1964, the one-time secretary was working for the newly founded pirate station, Radio Caroline, and modeling, albeit coyly, one of its promotional T-shirts.

Brian Jones, "the longest-haired Stone of them all," exercised a certain diplomacy when he shared the news with reporters: "I didn't like the number when I heard it on the radio, but I like it now." In fact, some suggested that the song, one of a handful taped at the Chess recording studios back in June, was too country influenced, just too damn pleasant, to meet the requirements of those frenzy-seeking Stones fans. Jagger, meanwhile, was apparently nonplussed by the news: "I don't care a damn whether our new record has reached No. 1 … what's it matter anyway?"

News of the single's success was soon eclipsed by the band's appearance on BBC-TV's leading pop show, *Juke Box Jury*. Inevitably, perhaps, the panel of R&B enthusiasts found little of positive note to report on a succession of new singles, much to the annoyance of host David Jacobs. Even Elvis Presley didn't get any praise from the group, who claimed that the King of Rock had had his day.

The man from the *Daily Sketch* was not amused: "I report with no regret the death of a sacred cow on TV. A group of Neanderthal young men who call

chartbusters

themselves the Rolling Stones sat in judgment as the jury men. It was a mockery of a trial as the gum-chewing, ill-mannered, ill-humoured, illiberal, and illogical jurors indicated their pleasure or displeasure by catarrhal grunts that an ear, trained in the illiterate school of young people, could sometimes distinguish as, 'Well, yeah, er, I, er, mean, like, well it's, ha-ha, awful then. Naw, definitely not, in'it?' " For a band now

above The Stones notoriously shunned clichéd photo opportunities, but with the rest of the band away, Brian Jones went along with this "On top of the world" shot to celebrate the group's first No. 1 hit on July 6, 1964.

far left Miss, miss, miss! When the Stones showed little enthusiasm for the latest batch of new singles on BBC-TV's *Juke Box Jury*, prerecorded on June 27, 1964, they received a torrent of media abuse.

actively cultivating a rebellious image, it was tremendous publicity—and free, too.

The furore set the mood for the Stones' next round of live dates, which instantly turned ugly at the Empress Ballroom, Blackpool, England, when what was described as "Britain's biggest rock riot ever" ended with thirty fans being injured, £4,000 worth of damage, and four people in court. In fact, it wasn't fans who caused the damage, but a crowd of vacationing Scotsmen who objected to Brian Jones' on-stage antics. That night, the innocence of the Stones' early thrust for glory had been lost.

"It was a mockery of a trial as the gum-chewing, ill-mannered, ill-humoured, illiberal, and illogical jurors indicated their pleasure or displeasure by catarrhal grunts."

Daily Sketch

the new pop aristocracy

"A delightful day. It was the best-controlled large crowd we have had at Longleat. So few hospital cases ... "

the Marquess of Bath

ESPITE COMING ON with an attitude that many took to be virtually insurrectionary, the Rolling Stones were soon courted by the aristocracy, especially debutantes for whom a dalliance with pop's leading rogues would be seen as derring-do of the first order.

The first public evidence of this unlikely alliance came in August 1964 when the reportedly hip and "with-it" Marquess of Bath invited the Stones to headline the third open-air pop concert at his Longleat House stately home near Warminster in Wiltshire, England. To demonstrate his enthusiasm for the new beat group craze—which it was in August 1964—the 59-year-old marquess donned a long black wig and sang a few words into a microphone to the 16,000-strong audience. "Just a bit of damn silly fun," he quipped.

But it was the Rolling Stones the crowd, some of whom had lined up all night, had

come to see. Unfortunately, their arrival prompted the inevitable disturbances. Eager to gain a closer view of the band, the audience surged forward into the crash barriers. A reported 200 of them fainted, each one of them passed overhead on a "conveyor-belt" system into the arms of police and ambulancemen and then taken on stretchers to the relative tranquillity of Longleat gardens.

The marquess, who held a reception for the Stones before they took to the stage, didn't let this spoil his fun: "A delightful day. It was the best-controlled large crowd we have had at Longleat. So few hospital cases— the fans were wonderful." He might well have been pleased, but to the authorities and media, the Longleat concert was farther evidence that the Rolling Stones spelled trouble.

The event, and its problems, wasn't the only trouble spot that weekend. The following Monday's headlines were dominated by the so-called "Battle of Hastings," where a series of skirmishes between Mods and Rockers at the Sussex seaside resort was only controlled when a riot squad was flown in from Scotland Yard in London. Those arrested were detained in Lewes Prison, an unwelcoming residence that would later play host to a more infamous guest …

facing page and above August 2, 1964: After a personal guided tour of Longleat House, the Rolling Stones walked out onto a most unlikely stage—the imposing flight of steps at the front of the house.

left An image of devotion and despair in one frame. It was common practice for music fans to bring home-made posters and badges to early pop concerts. Unfortunately, the sight of fainting fans being carried away was equally familiar.

he
told
'em

Oldham

"I didn't come into the pop business just to make money. Success—that's everything. When I do something it has to be 100 percent properly done, or nothing ... "

Andrew Oldham

facing page Andrew Oldham was the first of a new breed of pop managers—hip, young and creatively-minded. At 20, he was even younger than the band he represented.

left September 16, 1964: Andrew Oldham and Sheila Klein toast their wedding after a secret ceremony at a Glasgow Registry Office in Scotland. The bride drank tomato juice, while the groom opted for a decidedly sober orange juice.

above left After catching a plane back to London, the newlyweds called in on the 18-year-old bride's parents in Hampstead. Her mother told reporters: "We thought she was too young to marry."

ANDREW "LOOG" OLDHAM was crucial to the Rolling Stones' early success. He took them from playing dingy backrooms in the suburbs of London to international stardom. In feeding the press with sensational slogans, including the infamous "Would you let your sister go out with a Rolling Stone?," he did much to fashion the group's bad boy image.

After witnessing the Stones at the Crawdaddy Club in suburban Richmond in April 1963, Oldham, then a small-time publicist, moved quickly. Within a week, he'd signed the band to a management deal, sacked "sixth Stone" pianist Ian Stewart, and secured them a deal with Decca Records. He also nominated himself as the band's record producer—despite having no experience.

Oldham's first great achievement was selling the Rolling Stones to the world. His second was creating the songwriting partnership of Mick Jagger and Keith Richard. Most of the band's early records had been cover versions of American blues and R&B material. Oldham understood that for the Stones to properly rival the Beatles, and, lest we forget, reap those lucrative publishing royalties, they'd have to write their own songs. He forced the pair into a room and told them not to come out until they'd written one. It worked.

It wasn't long before the partnership began to gel, although one of the first Jagger/Richard songs, "As Tears Go By," ended up with another of Oldham's protégées, Marianne Faithfull. By the time this was released, in August 1964, Oldham was already widening his empire, producing Jagger/Richard-penned singles for George Bean, Adrienne Poster, the Mighty Avengers, and Gene Pitney. Inevitably, he was already talking about setting up his own record company.

a shaggy-mane story

THE ROLLING STONES' long and enduring association with the British justice system got underway with a couple of relatively low-key cases involving Mick Jagger. Both resulted in small fines for traffic offenses, but they also provided a taste of things to come.

The first case arose from an incident on April 30, 1964 when, prior to a concert at the Majestic Ballroom in Birkenhead, England, the Stones had driven up early on what was described by Jagger's solicitor as "an errand of mercy." Two fans who'd intended to catch the show had been involved in a car accident and the band were

> "Put out of your minds this nonsense talked about these young men. They are not long-haired idiots, but highly intelligent university men."
>
> **Mr. Dale Parkinson**

on their way in Mick's Ford Consul to pay them a surprise visit. It wasn't a good day: The show was abandoned after fans invaded the stage, and Jagger was charged with driving without insurance and at a speed of up to 50 m.p.h. in a 30 m.p.h. zone.

As a soberly dressed Jagger sat quietly in the Liverpool court on August 10, his lawyer Mr. Dale Parkinson told the magistrates: "These young people do not live in the same world as you or I. They are probably thinking of the next tune they are going to make. Here is a famous artist who was not insured because he did not have enough time." Invoking Jagger's "fine background," he added that his client "is very worried and upset that he is before the court." The

chairman of the court Mr. R. L. Martindale fined Jagger £32 and endorsed his driving license twice (similar to receiving points).

Unbeknown to the court, Mick had already been charged with similar traffic offenses on April 18, while driving through Wolverhampton on the way back from a gig in Chester. This case finally came to court on November 26, shortly after the band had

returned from a second, far more successful visit to the United States.

On this second occasion in court, his lawyer invoked the great hero of Blenheim, the Duke of Marlborough, as a way of deflecting any possible prejudice against the controversial Stone. The Duke "had longer hair than my client," claimed Mr. Parkinson. "His hair was powdered, I think, because of

below November 26, 1964: A somber-suited Mick leaves the court at Tettenhall, Staffordshire, after being found guilty of three traffic offenses. He'd just heard the names of the Duke of Marlborough and Emperor Caesar Augustus cited as part of his defense.

Liverpool only counted as one, Mick was able to retain his license, thus assuring his, and the band's, continued ability to earn "invisible" income for the nation.

Meanwhile, the Stones received a welcome fillip on September 8 when news that they had ousted the Beatles as Britain's No. 1 vocal and instrumental group in a poll of *Melody Maker* readers made the front pages of the national press. Voting was close in what was described as a "battle of the mop-hairs."

The news only served to encourage their fans' enthusiasm. During August, a concert in Amsterdam ended after ten minutes when seats were ripped up and the stage invaded. A show in St. Helier, Jersey, was constantly interrupted by running battles and ugly scuffles with overzealous security men. By the time the Stones set off for their fourth British tour on September 5, they had taken to arriving at shows accompanied by police escorts. The *Melody Maker*'s "Police Riot Squads Ready for Action" story wasn't far from the truth. Everywhere they went, the Rolling Stones were greeted by traumatic scenes—chanting crowds, sobbing girls, jealous boyfriends, and the occasional stray air-gun pellet.

above The only people to greet Mick's arrival at Tettenhall Magistrates Court were three press photographers and two policemen. But later when he walked through the town, he was spotted by a middle-aged woman "who leapt from a van and demanded his autograph,"

left August 10, 1964: According to his lawyer Mr. Dale Parkinson (right), Jagger was an "extremely intelligent, charming, and delightful young man." However, he still received a £32 fine for traffic offenses in his first court case, held in Liverpool.

below September 13, 1964: Stonesmania got serious throughout the incident-spattered fall 1964 tour. This scene, where the band make a dash for the stage door while police keep the fans at bay, was typical.

fleas. My client has no fleas." Besides, he appealed to the magistrates: "Put out of your minds this nonsense talked about these young men. They are not long-haired idiots, but highly intelligent university men." In truth, only Jagger had attended

college, at the renowned London School of Economics, but he failed to graduate due to band commitments.

The court chairman Mr. Jack Bradburn fined Jagger £16 and endorsed his license. But in ruling that the two endorsements at

FANDEMONIUM!

"The sight and sound of the Rolling Stones often did strange things to otherwise sensible teenage girls."

left September 14, 1964: Not all Stones fans came at them with scissors or fists. Alison Anderson (left) and Elizabeth Sayers (right), both 16, pictured back-stage at the ABC Theatre, Chester, were rewarded for their good behavior with a set of autographs, some posed shots with the band, and two tickets for the evening performance.

facing page, below left December 29, 1964: The quietest month of the group's career to date ended when *Daily Mirror* showbiz reporter Don Short arranged for three vacationing Dutch fans to visit Mick Jagger in his Hampstead, London, flat. They'd broken away from their sightseeing party in the hope of tracking the band down and, in desper-ation, had contacted the *Mirror* man. Enjoying a coffee with Mick are (left to right) Tonny Intvem (19), her sister Anja (15), and Els Meppelder (19).

Chapter Two 1965—66
SWINGING LONDON

DURING 1965 AND 1966, the Rolling Stones consolidated their position as chief rivals to the Beatles, in the face of stiff competition from emerging groups like the Who, the Kinks, the Animals, and Them. Their expressions grew ever more surly, their concerts more riotous, and their records sounded increasingly like clarion calls to teenage revolution. With other groups taking up the cause of rhythm and blues, the Stones sought to expand their musical repertoire, drawing heavily on contemporary American sounds and, increasingly, on the fast-maturing songwriting partnership of Mick Jagger and Keith Richard.

The results were dramatic. While their earlier blues and R&B covers established the group as malcontents keen to associate themselves with the unvarnished and heavy rhythms of black America, the new Jagger/Richard songs became instant anthems for a newly confident generation of teenagers. It was as if the rapid changes of the modern world were being measured out in pop hits—from the cool assurance of "The Last Time," early in 1965, to the mocking arrogance of "(I Can't Get No) Satisfaction" and "Get Off Of My Cloud" later in the same year.

By 1966, gaps in their hectic schedule had given the Stones time to consider what was happening to them—and their contemporaries. Young lives were now being roused by discontent at the "old ways" and a new-found thirst for experimentation, and this was clearly reflected in Jagger/Richard's latest, more radical hits, like "19th Nervous Breakdown," "Paint It Black," and the thrilling, cacophonous "Have You Seen Your Mother, Baby, Standing In The Shadow." So much had changed, and so quickly. ■

> "Their expressions grew ever more surly, their concerts more riotous, and their records sounded increasingly like clarion calls to teenage revolution."

left September 28, 1966: It was a new-look dandyfied Stones that posed with two young fans—sisters Kathryn Brennan (left), 14, and Judy Brennan (right), 15—on the steps of the band's Manchester hotel.

1965–66

we want the Stones!

The Stones are banned from a Yorkshire hotel in March 1965 after leaving their rooms in what the manager described to the *Daily Mirror* as "a terrible state. One of the rooms had phone numbers scribbled on the walls, and biscuits [cookies] had been trodden into the carpet." The receptionist, "pretty German-born Mrs. Heidi Smith, 25," added: "It was disgusting. They used bad language and were very rude to the staff." The Stones deny the claims.

The group's fave raves in '65, as revealed on *Ready, Steady, Go!* are: Wilson Pickett's "In The Midnight Hour" (Mick); Bob Dylan's "Like A Rolling Stone" (Keith); the Four Tops' "The Same Old Song" (Brian); Bo Diddley's "Hey Good Lookin'" (Bill); and Ramsay Lewis Trio's "The In Crowd" (Charlie).

The perils of wearing a tie, revealed by Mick Jagger: "It's something extra to which a fan can hang when you are trying to get in and out of a theatre," he tells the *Daily Mirror* in March 1965.

When Mick, Brian, and Bill are fined £5 each on July 22, 1965 for urinating against a garage wall in East London, the magistrate tells them: "Just because you have reached an exalted height in your profession, it does not mean you can behave in this manner."

Brian Jones is usually the first to fall ill on tour, but in December 1965 Keith Richard has the closest scrape with death after being electrocuted on stage at a concert in Sacramento, California. He is reportedly saved only because he was wearing a pair of Hush Puppies shoes.

"I just can't cope anymore," Andrew Oldham tells the *Daily Mirror* in August 1966. "Worrying about the Stones' private lives has given me ulcers. I shall carry on making their records, but what they do out of the studio will be none of my concern." Oldham, who insists he'll break away from the team in two weeks' time, adds: "Furthermore, I want no part of managing anybody else."

Maverick Labour MP Tom Driberg defends the Stones in parliament in July 1966, after a magistrate described the group as "complete morons" who "wear filthy clothes and act like clowns."

above One policeman manages to remain good-humored about the scenes that greeted the Stones' performance at the ABC Theatre in Belfast on January 6, 1965.

1965 BEGAN MUCH AS the previous year had done—with the Rolling Stones on the road. On January 6, they played two shows at the ABC Theatre in Belfast, the first date on a short Irish tour. Support acts included a young girl singer called Twinkle, who wore Stones-like striped shirts and carried a whiff of the band's rebellious spirit about her. But it was the Stones who the crowds had come to see, and the performances were greeted by the usual scenes of over-enthusiasm. Bill Wyman recalls the variety of dangerous objects that were hurled toward the stage—ashtrays, an iron bolt, and a girl's patent-leather shoe.

When the Stones returned to Ireland in September, manager Andrew Oldham invited along a young, talented moviemaker named Peter Whitehead. Mixing dramatic concert footage and revealing interviews with each Stones member, his resulting film, *Charlie Is My Darling*, remains one of the great lost Stones artifacts. One day, this fabulous, fly-on-the-wall insight into life as a Rolling Stone during the hyperactive mid-sixties will be granted a release. But not, apparently, for the foreseeable future.

The January tour of Ireland was followed by a substantial visit to Australasia and the Far East, another jaunt around Britain in March, then mainland Europe, Canada and North America, Scotland and Scandinavia, and back again to Britain for a string of dates between July and October, with a short break during August. Then it

" '(I Can't Get No) Satisfaction,' with its insistent, ringing fuzz guitar riff, coupled with its perfect Angry Young Man lyric, sounded like a manifesto for imminent cultural revolution."

was back to North America for the remaining months of 1965.

Amazingly enough, the Stones still managed to release two albums during the year. Neither signified a huge advance on their debut LP. *The Rolling Stones No. 2*, issued in January, augmented the inevitable Chuck Berry numbers with notable dips into the contemporary sound of black America, via covers of Otis Redding and Solomon Burke material. Just three Jagger/Richard songs made it to the final cut, all easily identified by their brattish lyrics and somewhat ham-fisted delivery.

The album's mild conservatism was all the more surprising because, in terms of singles, the group moved forward with great strides. In February, the coupling of two Jagger/Richard originals, "The Last Time" and "Play With Fire," encapsulated the new songwriting team's contrasting pop/ballad styles. "The Last Time" sounded dynamic, electric, and more original than the derivative fare the pair had been writing for the LP; "Play With Fire" was a beautiful ballad drenched in bitter melancholy and quite unique.

The single/album dichotomy was repeated later in the year. When "(I Can't Get No) Satisfaction" was released in August, its insistent, ringing fuzz guitar riff, coupled with its perfect Angry Young Man lyric, sounded like a manifesto for imminent cultural revolution. Yet, two weeks later, the band's third LP, *Out Of Our Heads*, failed to live up to expectations—either of its title or of the preceding 45.

Thankfully, when 1966 arrived, and gaps began to appear in the band's grueling concert schedule, the Stones were able to adopt a more considered approach to their albums, too. The benefits were instant: The *Aftermath* album, issued in April that year, was an all Jagger/Richard collection that sounded remarkably sophisticated compared to the band's previous LPs. From that moment, the Rolling Stones regarded recording as at least as important as live performance. More crucially, they'd begun to regard it as something of an art.

right It was all smiles backstage, but when the curtain went up, the group were bombarded with dangerous objects as the crowd's enthusiasm threatened to get out of control.

satisfaction guaranteed ?

above July 7, 1965: Manager Andrew Oldham (center) on his way to Wells Street Court, central London, on a traffic charge. With him (far right) is Reg Stiles, his chauffeur.

right August 27, 1965: On the twenty-seventh floor of London's Hilton Hotel, Allen Klein and Andrew Oldham celebrate a deal which, according to reports, will guarantee the Rolling Stones "$3 million over the next five years." Hmm …

"Under the terms of a deal concluded with our American business manager, Mr. Allen Klein, the Stones are guaranteed $3 million over the next five years."

Andrew Oldham

above August 23, 1965: After being made up for an appearance on Granada TV's *Scene At 6.30*, the Stones went to a nearby window to peer down on girl fans below. They performed their latest single, "(I Can't Get No) Satisfaction," on the show.

left Police and doormen are forced to restrain a crowd of 200 fans who broke through a barrier at the Manchester studios while the Stones were inside filming.

INTEREST IN the Rolling Stones inevitably led reporters to find out more about their wives and girlfriends. With both Bill Wyman and Charlie Watts quietly married (to Diane and Shirley respectively), and Keith Richard seemingly content to concentrate on his guitar-playing and songwriting skills at this stage in his career, attention focused on the love lives of the two most popular Stones, Mick Jagger and Brian Jones.

When the Stones began to spend more time out of the country than in it, Jagger's girlfriend Chrissie Shrimpton became the subject of magazine and newspaper profiles. Her loyalty to Mick was such that she rarely discussed their relationship in any meaningful

"Chrissie Shrimpton displayed a distinctly bohemian streak when she said: 'I'm just not ambitious, I guess. I'm not interested in money.'"

this page May 12, 1965: Chrissie Shrimpton, of whom it was reported: "What with being known as either Jean Shrimpton's sister or Mick Jagger's bird, life was unbearable."

she smiled sweetly

By the end of 1965, three former girlfriends had claimed that Brian Jones had fathered their children, although only Linda Lawrence, his regular girlfriend since 1963, received any official acknowledgment. Jones met her when the Stones played the Ricky Tick club in Linda's hometown of Windsor, in England, several months before the group found fame. She was 16, she cut his hair, nursed his easily bruised ego, and her parents, Violet and Alex, invited the Stone to share their house with them. But the birth of a son, Julian, in 1964, complicated matters. Only after the threat of legal action in August 1965 did the prurient Stone make an out-of-court settlement with Linda.

Inspired by Linda Lawrence's action, another girl, Dawn Molloy, made a similar claim shortly afterward, with a little help from her mother, Joyce. She produced a locket that revealed two photographs—one of her with Brian, the other of baby Paul Andrew. Months later, in January 1966, it was reported that 21-year-old Pat Andrews of South London had lodged a paternity claim for her son Julian Mark in a London court.

1965 had also been the year that women saw a bit of pop action of their own. On May 13, the *Daily Mirror*'s pop pundit Patrick Doncaster reported that: "Girls are making a lot of noise again. Eleven of 'em are in this week's Pop Thirty ... And more on the way." On the up were Jackie Trent, Sandie Shaw, Anita Harris, Jackie de Shannon, Joan Baez, and a young convent-educated singer from Reading, England, Marianne Faithfull. This "aristocratic lady" had created headlines ever since scoring her first hit the previous summer with her version of Jagger/Richard's "As Tears Go By." Her love life, too, had been carefully pored over, although the announcement, on March 10, 1965, that she had become engaged to Cambridge art student John Dunbar, put a temporary lid on that. Gene Pitney, her touring costar, had been the subject of most rumors, but as she twisted her £50 Georgian engagement ring on her finger, she told reporters: "I know what has been said about Gene and I, but there was never anything in it."

above August 31, 1965: A locket featuring photos of Brian Jones and baby Paul Andrew accompanied Dawn Molloy's claim the Stone was the father of her child.

top far left April 27, 1965: Brian's girlfriend Linda Lawrence, pictured at home with one of his gold disks, his fan mail, and a poodle dog "Pip," a gift from Jones.

top left Left holding the baby: Linda Lawrence in August 1965 with Julian, her year-old son by Brian Jones. A copy of the Stones' first album can be seen in the background.

left February 24, 1965: Chrissie Shrimpton (center) was roped in to publicize the Toggery Five's latest record, "I'd Much Rather Be With The Boys." The connection? The song was written by Mick Jagger and Keith Richard.

detail. When she did let her defenses drop, it was only to impart obvious quips like, "I always liked more unconventional boys; that's why I like Mick, I guess."

However, Chrissie did reveal her fears about living life in the public eye. "Sometimes I get very screwed up with all [Mick's] fans hating me," she told Marjorie Proops of the *Daily Mirror* in a profile titled "The Kid Sister" in May 1965. "Then I decided it was time I got a bit conceited. I went around telling everyone what a strong powerful character I'd got," she added. But Chrissie's vulnerabilities just kept tumbling out. Her sister Jean was always "so good at everything ... beautiful ... always prettier than me and good at sport. I was always jealous of her when we were young, because she was the favorite at home and I think when I was born they wanted a boy." Chrissie also displayed a distinctly bohemian streak when she told Proops: "I'm just not ambitious, I guess. I'm not interested in money."

"Chrissie Shrimpton's boyfriend, Rolling Stone Mick Jagger, in a beige denim suit and violet shirt, was best man." *Daily Mirror*

top (left to right) Art gallery owner Robert Fraser, his girlfriend Deborah Dixon, Linda Lawrence, and Brian Jones, celebrate Fraser's birthday in a Tangier nightclub in September 1965.

above left June 2, 1966: Keith Richard steps out with 26-year-old Canadian model Kari-Ann Möller at the premiere of Roman Polanski's *Cul-de-Sac* at the Cameo Poly, Regent Street, London.

above middle August 18, 1965: Mick Jagger and Chrissie Shrimpton pictured at the party to celebrate "the zaniest wedding of '65." Getting spliced were Swinging Sixties photographer David

above right October 3, 1965: The grim reality of foiling fans with elaborate plans and decoy vans was rarely far away. "Who thought of this— Montgomery?," joked Jagger as the

facing page September 8, 1965: Mick, Keith and Charlie try their luck on a roulette table in Douglas on the Isle of Man, following a concert. Brian was reportedly "composing and resting;"

good times

smash hit

"When I'm driving in my car, and some man comes on the radio ..."

September 28, 1966: Mick Jagger and Chrissie Shrimpton narrowly escape injury when Mick's £5,000 midnight-blue Aston Martin DB6 was involved in a collision with a Ford Anglia belonging to the Countess of Carlisle in central London, near his Marylebone flat. No one was hurt, but Jagger was none too happy: "I only bought the car three months ago," he said. "The damage is going to cost about £200."

hysteria at the Albert Hall

THE STONES KICKED OFF their first British tour in a year (and their last until 1971) with a show at London's Royal Albert Hall on September 23, 1966, which proved neither they, nor their audiences, had grown any tamer. Screaming fans stormed the stage, knocked Keith Richard to the ground, and almost strangled Mick Jagger. Keith wasn't unduly concerned: "We were in danger of becoming 'respectable.' But now the new wave [of fans] has arrived, rushing the stage just like old times." More than fifty girls were taken to hospital after a series of stage invasions.

The line-up for the tour was particularly strong, with R&B rivals the Yardbirds and visiting American soul act the Ike & Tina Turner Revue among the supporting acts. Meanwhile, the Stones' own performance was growing more menacing, as they began to introduce some of their more adventurous material into the set. Added to crowd-pleasers such as "Not Fade Away" and "Time Is On My Side" were recent hits including their latest 45, "Have You Seen Your Mother, Baby, Standing In The Shadow."

Like the Beatles, by 1966, the Stones began to have trouble reproducing their records on stage. Recording techniques (and the sound effects both had started to use) had become more sophisticated. On top of that, the Stones were no longer the R&B purists they were back in 1963 and 1964. Their music had changed so much that by the time of their fourth LP, *Aftermath*, issued in April 1966, every song was a Jagger/Richard original. Of those, only one, "Goin' Home," could be regarded as an R&B song, and even that barrier-breaking, 11-minute-plus cut had as much in common with jazz improvization as it did with 12-bar blues.

right Bill, Keith, Brian, Charlie, and Mick backstage at the band's infamous Royal Albert Hall show. Jones had cracked two bones in his wrist while in Tangier, hence his bandaged hand.

"We were in danger of becoming 'respectable.'"

Keith Richard

right Guitarist Brian Jones strikes another B-flat chord. The bob-haired Stone was experimenting increasingly with other instruments, including sitar, marimba, dulcimer, and recorder, adding distinctive and exotic textures to the Rolling Stones' sound.

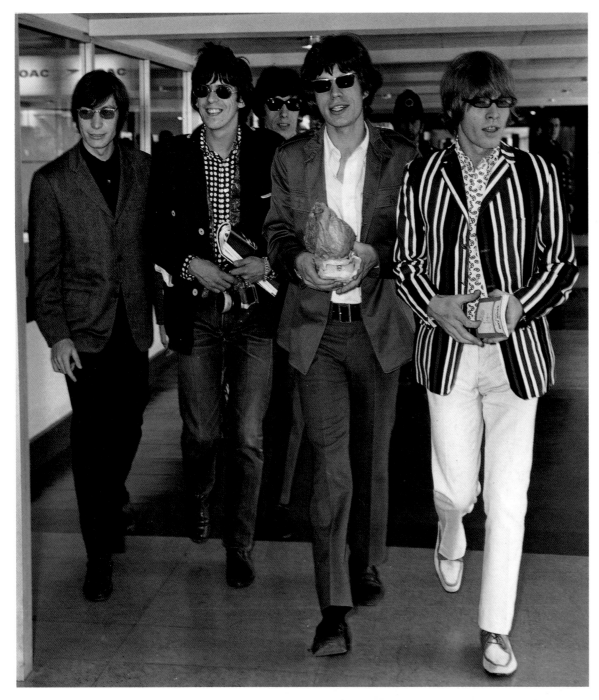

"A CELEBRITY IS SOMEONE who gets photographed every time they walk through an airport," Rolling Stones' manager Andrew Oldham once claimed. As the group's international popularity flourished, and their desires to escape the grueling merry-go-round of tours, television appearances, and recording sessions were increasingly granted, the Stones spent much of the middle years of the Swinging Sixties in the air.

ride on, baby

In addition to their regular tours of the United States, Australia, and mainland Europe, the Stones had also joined the international jet-set, flying off to spend weekends in Paris (Mick and Chrissie Shrimpton's preferred romantic destination) or Morocco, where Brian Jones found solace away from the relentless pressure of being a Rolling Stone. According to Linda Lawrence, his one-time girlfriend, "Morocco was a place where he could forget all that had happened back in England."

By late 1965, Brian had fallen in love with Anita Pallenberg, a stunning and educated, Italian-born model. Their relationship was, like Brian's within the group, unsettled and largely dependent on the Stone's ever-changing moods, but her worldliness and strong character was more

above The Stones fly off to America for a month-long tour on June 23, 1966. News that fourteen New York hotels had refused to accommodate the Stones obviously concerned Brian Jones, who clutches a copy of *The Good Loo Guide*.

right Chrissie Shrimpton flies out to Los Angeles on December 4, 1965 to join Mick at the end of the Stones' American tour. She wears "a dark gray suit with the four inches above the knee hemline made so familiar by her older sister".

far right December 4, 1966: Marianne Faithfull, shortly before her relationship with Mick Jagger becomes public. She had hoped to meet a French movie producer at the National Film Theatre, but he failed to turn up.

than a match for Brian. He'd met her backstage at a Stones' show in Munich, West Germany, on September 14, 1965, around the time his relationship with Linda Lawrence was crumbling. By the end of the year, there was already talk of marriage.

But the monogamous life did not come easily to Brian. It was only in May 1966 that he invited Anita to share his London flat in Courtfield Road with him. By the end of the year, during which time the couple had grown even more similar in style,

tales of their fractious relationship were legion: One vacation in Morocco ended with Brian returning with his arm in plaster after a particularly fiery altercation. Brian had strayed again, this time into the arms of Marianne Faithfull.

Marianne, who had also slept with Keith Richard around this time, had been on the periphery of the Stones' entourage since March 1964, when Andrew Oldham spotted her at a party and decided she had star quality. Her first single, "As Tears Go By," had been a huge hit, and despite her marriage and child, she managed to maintain a successful singing career. Although she initially found the Stones "crass and boorish", Marianne had grown tired of her domestic lifestyle and had begun to drop in at Jones' flat to sample the decadent world of the Rolling Stones at first hand. After a Stones show at Colston Hall, Bristol, on October 7, 1966, Marianne Faithfull and Mick Jagger became entwined in an affair that would soon become the pop romance of the decade.

Meanwhile, Jagger's relationship with Chrissie Shrimpton had deteriorated badly. On December 15, the pair had planned to fly to Jamaica for Christmas, but Jagger canceled the tickets and instead spent the day in London with Marianne, having lunch in Knightsbridge before shopping for presents in Harrods department store in the afternoon. Shortly before Christmas, Jagger told Chrissie their relationship was over, and on Christmas Eve her belongings were removed from their shared flat in Harley House, Marylebone Road, and Marianne was quickly moved in, together with her young son, Nicholas.

Mick explained the situation to the press as he posed alone in a Soho restaurant: "We just couldn't get along together, for two people so close to one another. Three years is a long time to be with someone, but I don't feel as cut up about it as you may imagine." At this stage, no mention was made of his secret trysts with Marianne.

From her parents' home in Burnham, Buckinghamshire, Chrissie put on a brave face: "We just grew out of each other. This was the only solution." She said that her immediate plan was to go to drama training school, but a few days later, she'd been admitted to Greenway Nursing Home in London, suffering from the effects of stress. Her next boyfriend was Small Faces singer Steve Marriott.

far left Brian Jones meets actress and girlfriend Anita Pallenberg, who has just flown in from Munich on December 3, 1966. The pair are working on a movie, *A Degree of Murder*, for which Jones is scoring the soundtrack.

left December 23, 1966: Dinner for one at the Trattoria Terrazza Italian restaurant in Soho, London, as Mick declares his romance with Chrissie Shrimpton is over. "I don't dig the marriage bit at the moment," he added.

"At a recent Chelsea party, Jones said 'the wedding is definitely on, and Bob Dylan will be the best man.'"

New Musical Express

Chapter Three 1967
STONED ... BUSTED!

1967 WAS THE YEAR all the Rolling Stones' "bad-boy" publicity rebounded on them. A series of drug busts threatened to break the band, either by landing them in jail, or else by creating a climate of fear and paranoia that could have sapped their spirit. It almost worked. The hits dried up, as did the concert appearances. They lost their influential manager. To cap it all, a new, essentially American youth movement, centered on hippies and psychedelic fashions, threatened to render them obsolete. But the Stones proved remarkably resilient.

There has always been a strong suspicion that the Rolling Stones had been singled out as a convenient scapegoat by sinister establishment forces who held them at least partially responsible for the new-found permissiveness that threatened to undermine British morality. It's by no means far-fetched: The first drug bust was a carefully planned exercise involving the collusion of the police with a well-known national newspaper, and at least two of the band claimed they were being kept under police surveillance.

> ## "One doesn't ask for responsibilities. Society has pushed me into this position ..."
> **Mick Jagger**

By the end of the year, the pressure had clearly got to Brian Jones, whose court appearances were being punctuated by recuperative visits to private clinics. His ability to fight back weakened by his diminished role in the group, and losing girlfriend Anita Pallenberg to Keith Richard, Jones appeared to have been earmarked for persecution. The most simple cure for his fears was to blot them out with the drink and drugs that served only to magnify his problems.

Ironically, as Mick Jagger was being hauled in front of the law courts, his fascination with the establishment grew stronger. His new partner Marianne Faithfull nurtured his thirst for culture, and when he wasn't leaving court in handcuffs, or attracting undue attention from burly customs officials at airports, he was likely to be found at theater and ballet premieres or scoffing canapés at literary parties. The Rolling Stones' music was conspicuous by its absence during 1967. ■

left May 10, 1967: Mick Jagger and Keith Richard are driven from Keith's house in West Wittering, Sussex, England, to the court where they were charged with various drug offenses. The Stones' drug battles dominated 1967.

1967

Police used batons and tear gas on 2,000 fans who stormed the Palace of Culture in Warsaw in an attempt to see the band's first performance behind the Iron Curtain.

Brian Jones' only publicly aired songwriting was used for the soundtrack of an obscure movie, *A Degree of Murder*. The movie was Germany's entry for the 1967 Cannes Film Festival.

A *Times* editorial concluded "Mr. Jagger received a more severe sentence [for possession of drugs] than would have been thought proper for any purely anonymous young man."

The Stones' friendly rivalry with the Beatles scaled new heights during 1967. Hidden among the flowers on the *Satanic Majesties* album were the heads of John, Paul, George, and Ringo. It was also a tacit acknowledgment of the Beatles' support during this chaotic year.

During the drugs case against Keith Richard, much was made in court about the unnamed naked girl at the party which police busted. "All that she was wearing was a light-colored fur-skin rug, which, from time to time, she let fall, disclosing her nude body." The girl, later named as Marianne Faithfull, had been upstairs taking a bath.

With Jagger and Richard in jail, newspapers asked: Can the Stones survive a spell in the wilderness? "It would be unthinkable for the other three to carry on without them," an associate and close friend of the band told the *Daily Mirror*.

Judge Block, who jailed the two Stones in June, told a farmers' dinner in November: "We did our best, your fellow countrymen and I, and my fellow magistrates, to cut these Stones down to size. But alas, it was not to be because the Court of Criminal Appeal let them roll free." The Stones' spokesman Les Perrin said the speech was "deplorable."

According to the *Daily Mirror* in December, world sales of Rolling Stones records had reaped more than £42 million. But by the paper's calculations, the group would have pocketed less than £3 million between them—before tax, too.

just dandy

AFTER COMPLETING WORK on their fifth LP, *Between The Buttons*, the Stones emerged on January 11 with a press conference in London's Green Park, before flying to the States to record a spot on the influential *Ed Sullivan Show*. It was obvious just from looking at them that the suburban R&B enthusiasts had blossomed into something far more exotic. Sporting a curious mix of neatly cut, Regency-style clothing, topped with some brightly colored acquisitions from their trips abroad, the Rolling Stones now began to resemble five latter-day Beau Brummels.

This flouting of convention also found its way into the band's music. The first significant touch of flamboyance could be heard on "Paint It Black," the band's May 1966 single, which featured a sitar, a multi-stringed Eastern instrument played by Brian Jones. About the same time, album tracks like "Under My Thumb" and "Lady Jane" were delicately adorned with marimbas, harpsichord, and dulcimer. But it was the two LPs that book-ended 1967, *Between The Buttons* and *Their Satanic Majesties Request*, which best reflect the band's collective state of mind during this traumatic period.

Initially, *Between The Buttons* sounded inconsequential in comparison with previous Stones albums. The band hadn't yet jettisoned the three-minute pop format, but as guitars buzzed, odd sounds came to the fore unexpectedly, and the lyrics didn't really make too much sense, it was as if a

below and right Green Park, London, January 11, 1967: The shapes and sights of things to come. The Stones emulate the San Francisco hippie fashions that swept the world during 1967.

veil of secrecy had been thrown over the songs. One in particular, the stoned, comic "Something Happened To Me Yesterday," was particularly prescient in light of future developments—right down to Mick Jagger's "Evenin' all" quip, a parody of Sgt. Dixon, a popular British TV policeman.

That musical mood of detachment reached a thrilling climax in August when the Stones issued the most intriguing single of their career. "We Love You" could only ever have been released during that heady, drug-induced Summer of Love. Opening to the sound of prison doors banging, it defied pop convention with its sparse, mantralike lyrics, punishing rhythms and bizarre Eastern-influenced brass and manic Mellotron finale. Ostensibly a thank-you to fans who'd supported the band during their summer drug trials, "We Love You" became the Stones' least successful 45 since 1963. It certainly had no hope of emulating the success of its predecessor, the "Let's Spend The Night Together"/"Ruby Tuesday" coupling.

The band's flirtation with exotic sounds and music that bore little resemblance to the R&B that originally fueled them was expunged at the end of the year, with the release of *Their Satanic Majesties Request*. Housed in a costly, three-dimensional gate-fold sleeve, this magical record was—and remains—the black sheep in the Stones' career. Ostensibly the band's answer to the Beatles' celebrated *Sgt Pepper's Lonely Hearts Club Band* album issued that summer, it ended up sounding—and looking—like its deranged, unloved cousin. It soon became clear that the Stones' musical imagination was far removed from the cozy, almost Victorian world inhabited by the Beatles. The record, which took the best part of a year to make, was a concept album in all but name, and its otherworldly demeanor, tinged with satanic darkness, mirrored perfectly the group's inner yearning to flee their all-too earthly troubles for an imaginary landscape.

Between-song nonsense, including the sound of a man snoring and Cockney market traders, disrupted the idea of a conventional LP, but it was the songs that carried the germ of innovation farther. One, the shapeless "Sing This Altogether (See What Happens)," seemed to reflect the newly fashionable acid trip perfectly, a suggestion that was apparent throughout an LP that rejoiced in the iconography of drug-induced escape.

above January 12, 1967: The superstitious Keith Richard, Brian Jones, and Bill Wyman choose to fly to New York on the 12th to avoid making a journey on Friday the 13th. Mick Jagger, who is not superstitious, leaves on Friday the 13th, and walks under a ladder on his way to the aircraft. The previous night, he'd witnessed an early club show by newcomer Jimi Hendrix.

"The Stones' musical imagination was far removed from the cozy, almost Victorian world inhabited by the Beatles."

carousel
catastrophe

"Anyone who thought we were changing our image to suit a family audience was mistaken."

Mick Jagger

left Mick Jagger argues with manager Andrew Oldham and the band's recording engineer Glyn Johns (in striped jacket). "That revolving stage isn't an altar. It's a drag," he tells reporters. The Stones refuse to mount the revolving stage at the end of the London Palladium Show on January 22, 1967, causing a furore.

left Promoting their latest single, "Let's Spend The Night Together," at the Palladium in London. The band walked off as the revolving stage began to move, prompting the show's director Mr Albert Locke to protest: "Who do the Stones think they are?"

above (from top) The group backstage at the London Palladium; Brian Jones tries out his recorder in readiness for the unveiling of a new song, "Ruby Tuesday;" making a quick exit after the show.

top left Two weeks later, comedians Peter Cook and Dudley Moore poked fun at Jagger and put the Stones on the show's revolving stage, albeit in Gerald Scarfe-designed papier-mâché form.

above and right On February 5, 1967, the *News of the World* claimed Mick Jagger had confessed to taking LSD. That evening, the Stones performed on the *Eamonn Andrews Show*.

below and facing page Mick used the occasion to announce that he would be suing the newspaper for libel. Backstage, he faced a barrage of questions from an inquisitive press.

Jagger speaks out

"I am quite shocked that a responsible newspaper ... can publish such a defamatory article about me."
Mick Jagger

up, up and away

ON FEBRUARY 12, 1967, Mick Jagger, together with several of his chums, was enjoying a blissful Sunday away from London at Keith Richard's West Wittering country home, when eighteen police officers knocked at the door with a warrant to search the premises for drugs. Just over a week later, he was photographed arriving at London's Royal Opera House for a ballet premiere in the presence of royalty. Notoriety, it seemed, did little harm to Jagger's social aspirations, and as the year's events unfolded, he received considerable support from some surprising establishment quarters, including a supportive editorial in *The Times* newspaper.

Having declared live on the *Eamonn Andrews Show* he would be suing the *News of the World* for libel in the light of its inflammatory "Pop Stars and Drugs" article, Mick Jagger promptly did so two days later, on February 7. He spent the rest of the week dodging press reporters by working in the recording studio, before driving down to join Keith and a few friends for a weekend party. Beatle George Harrison was also a party guest, with his wife Patti, but suspiciously, it was only after they left that police swooped on the house in an 8 P.M. raid on Sunday evening, fueling speculation that the authorities were only interested in nailing the Stones.

Everyone was searched and a variety of samples, including sun-tan lotion and some Earl Grey tea, were taken away for analysis. However, one guest, the mysterious David Schneiderman, escaped close scrutiny, and when he fled the country a few days later, suspicions were raised that he had been a "plant" at the party. Certainly, the *News of the World* got its scoop the following Sunday when it announced: "Drugs Squad Raid Pop Stars Party." A week later, a small news item, headed "Yard Report on Stones Raid," appeared in the *Daily Mirror*, which referred to "articles and substances seized in a raid on a country house owned by pop star Keith Richard." Another month passed before the *Mirror* reported the story in full, and by this time, the paper was able to add that Mick and Keith had been summoned to appear in court on drug charges.

Inevitably, the Stones were keen to escape the attention and on February 25 the three most socially active Stones—Mick, Keith and Brian—fled Britain for the relative peace of Morocco. It was during this trip that the band were rocked by another drama, this time one of their own making. While driving through France with Tom Keylock, the Rolling Stones' minder and chauffeur, the simmering ménage à trois of Brian, Keith, and Anita Pallenberg fatefully resolved itself when Jones became ill and was hospitalized, leaving Keith and Anita to drive on together to Marbella, Spain. By the

below right February 27, 1967: Pressmen peer in through the windows of Keith Richard's cottage in West Wittering, Sussex, England. Two weeks earlier, the premises had been raided in the Stones' most infamous drug bust.

center February 23, 1967: Mick and Marianne arrive at the Royal Opera House for a ballet premiere starring Margot Fonteyn and Rudolph Nureyev. Their attendance made front-page news—because they were eight minutes late. (Mick's brother Chris lurks in the background.)

far right Also attending Roland Petit's *Paradise Lost* ballet premiere was Princess Margaret. The smoking, drinking royal dropped in backstage when the Stones returned for a series of concerts in 1976.

middle of March, Brian Jones was alone in Tangier, while Anita, widely regarded as the strongest woman ever to penetrate the Stones' camp, had switched her amorous attentions to Keith. Inevitably, the balance of power within the group shifted farther away from Jones.

Meanwhile, the repercussions from the drug bust became apparent midway through a European tour during March

"I'm fed up with all this about the drug scene. It bores me."

Mick Jagger

and April. When the band (minus Mick) arrived at Orly airport, Paris, on April 10, customs officials made a thorough inspection of their luggage before letting them into the country. Although it was evident they were looking for drugs, French customs claimed the real reason for the stringent searches was that the group had been included on an international "red list" of so-called communist sympathizers.

Speaking to reporters, Mick claimed: "We knew they would be searched. Someone from Interpol told me," before adding that he was "fed up with all this about the drug scene. It bores me."

above March 6, 1967: Mick Jagger, on his return flight home from Brussels, when he was met by Marianne Faithfull.

left and far left April 11, 1967: Jagger flies off to join the rest of the Stones in Paris.

calm before the storm

"Stones fans—see you in Chichester on May 10!"

graffiti sighted at London Underground stations

facing page April 18, 1967: Bedraggled! Mick, Brian, and Charlie return home after the Stones' spring European tour ended with a huge show at the Panathinaikos stadium in Athens, Greece.

above left April 14, 1967: Model Suki Poitier wears fashion designer Ossie Clark's Stones-inspired "Red Rooster" dress. The widow of Guinness heir Tara Browne—who was a close friend of the Stones— Suki became Brian Jones latest girlfriend.

above right April 18, 1967: Marianne Faithfull clutches the customary bouquet of flowers at the opening night of Chekhov's *Three Sisters* at the Royal Court Theatre, London. She plays the part of Irina.

left Leaving the theater after Marianne's performance, Mick Jagger is bundled into a car, closely followed by Prince Stanislaus Klossowski de Rola, alias "Stash." The Prince became a close member of the Stones' inner circle.

live at the witch trials

facing page Mick and Keith step out of the guitarist's Redlands cottage to a beautiful spring day—and a car waits to take them to the West Sussex Quarter Sessions court.

above This teenager wears his support for the two Stones on his lapel—although he might have served the cause better if he'd learned to spell marijuana correctly!

top right May 10, 1967: This unlikely looking crowd waits patiently outside the court for Jagger and Richard to arrive.

right A sober-looking Mick Jagger slips out the back exit of the court, thus managing to avoid the crowd.

far right May 11, 1967: Brian Jones, followed by the ever-present Stash, steps out of West London Magistrates Court after being remanded on bail. The pair had been arrested and charged with possession of Indian hemp the previous afternoon.

ON THE MORNING of May 10, 1967, Mick Jagger and Keith Richard, together with art dealer Robert Fraser, arrived at a Chichester courthouse to face drug charges arising from the Redlands bust. A reported 500 teenagers, some of whom had traveled down from London to lend their support, milled around the court. Inside, all three defendants were being committed to trial, each electing to be tried by jury.

The court heard that "a strange sweet smell" greeted police when they descended on Keith Richard's Tudor farmhouse in February, and it was claimed that the smell could have been incense used to cover hemp-smoking. Mr. Anthony McCowan, the prosecutor, said police had found a party in progress, with seven men and one woman in the house.

The case against each defendant was then outlined. Jagger, McCowan said, had been carrying a phial in his jacket containing four tablets. After analysis, these were found to contain a mixture of amphetamine sulfate and methylamphetamine hydrochloride. In Fraser's case, eight green capsules were found in his jacket, and twenty-four white tablets in his pants pocket. It was alleged these contained heroin and amphetamine hydrochloride. Keith Richard was alleged to be responsible for a briar pipe bowl found in his living room. Traces of hemp were also found on a living-room table and in an ashtray by a bedside.

Sgt. Stanley Cudmore alleged he said to Richard: "Should laboratory tests show dangerous drugs have been used on the premises and not related to any individual, you will be held responsible. I cautioned him and he replied: 'I see. They pin it all on me.' " Jagger was charged with possessing four tablets containing an illegal substance; Richard of allowing his premises to be used for smoking hemp.

Defending the two Rolling Stones, Mr. Geoffrey Leach said: "The defence deny most strongly these allegations, and challenge the interpretations sought to be placed by the prosecution on the evidence in their possession." Mick and Keith pleaded not guilty before they, together with Robert Fraser, were bound over for trial and given bail of £100.

As Jagger and Richard slipped away via the back door of the courtroom, police in London were preparing to raid Brian Jones' flat in Courtfield Road, South Kensington.

"Heroin Found at Stones Party Court is Told."

Daily Mirror

They turned up at 4 P.M. with a warrant and spent half-an-hour talking to Jones and 24-year-old "Swiss-born entertainer" Prince Stanislaus Klossowski de Rola, Baron de Wattville, before arresting them. The detectives also left with several bags containing material for analysis. Brian and "Stash" were taken to Kensington police station where they were charged with unlawful possession of drugs—approximately 50 grains of cannabis resin (hemp)—and bailed to appear at West London Magistrates Court the following day.

Wednesday May 10, 1967 had been an extraordinary day for the Rolling Stones—even by their standards. The following morning the country woke up to read newspaper headlines about two separate drug cases involving band members. While Mick and Keith's case made the front pages, the addition of the Jones charge helped foster a moral panic concerning drug use among young people.

At the court hearing later that day, Jones and Stash were let out for three weeks on £250 bail each. The *Daily Mirror* couldn't resist reporting on Brian's flamboyant attire: "Jones was wearing a white, lace-cuffed shirt, polka-dot 'kippered' tie, flared reefer jacket and blue bell-bottom trousers." The crowd didn't go unnoticed, either: "As he and de Rola left the court and walked to a silver Rolls-Royce, girls in a waiting crowd screamed: 'They're gorgeous!'."

The busts took their toll on the Stones, although they did manage to snatch a few days together in May to record a thank-you single for their fans, "We Love You." The Beatles offered moral support and dropped by to add backing vocals to the single. They also invited Mick and Brian to their own sessions, with Jagger sitting in on the recording of "All You Need Is Love" and Jones blowing sax on "You Know My Name (Look Up The Number)."

this and facing page This unusual session was shot at Olympic Studios, Barnes, in south London, on May 19, 1967. Mick Jagger (facing page) in the control room with engineer Glyn Johns, holds a fetching grimace for the *Daily Mirror* photographer.

top far right Andrew Oldham (with hat, center), maintained a presence at the session, but his role had diminished so much that on September 14, it was announced the Stones had "parted from [their] recording manager."

below right Keith Richard with Ian "Stu" Stewart, the Stones' original piano player, who remained an integral part of the band set-up until his death in 1985.

far right Brian Jones, dressed in what one headline described as: "The gear that grandma used to favor". He is pictured at his Mellotron, ready to add a demonic instrumental part to "We Love You."

on with the show

"The Rolling Stones have never been renowned for following trends. They tend to set their own trends instead."

Daily Mirror

four days that

shook the Stones

top far left June 29, 1967: Mick Jagger arrives at court handcuffed to co-defendant Robert Fraser (left) to hear the verdict. He'd spent the previous two nights locked up in Lewes Prison.

top center June 28, 1967: Marianne Faithfull, alias the unnamed "nude girl in a merry mood at Stones party," waits in a nearby hotel for the conclusion of the case against Mick and Keith.

top left June 29, 1967: Keith Richard signs an autograph outside the court as he arrives to hear the outcome of the case. He was found guilty and sentenced to one year in prison with £500 costs.

below far left June 29, 1967: two West Sussex women police officers, Rosemary Slade (left) and Evelyn Fuller, arrive at the Chichester court. Both were involved in the police raid on Redlands Cottage.

below center After the verdicts, Mick was transferred to Brixton Prison, while Keith spent a night here, in Wormwood Scrubs, before being released the following day.

left 30 June 1967: "It's great to be out!" Leaving Wormwood Scrubs, after Mick had arrived there from Brixton Prison in a Rolls Bentley to pick up Keith. Both had been granted bail.

right 4 July 1967: Mick and Keith in defiant mood in the garden at Redlands. Three days earlier, *The Times* newspaper had published an impassioned defense, and within a month, their sentences had been quashed.

"When Jagger was asked what the tablets were for, he replied: 'To stay awake at work.'"

Daily Mirror

BETWEEN JUNE 27 AND 30, Mick Jagger and Keith Richard were found guilty of drug charges, locked up in jail, and then released pending appeals that looked likely to hang over them until late October. Mercifully, the hearings were brought forward to the end of July, and the successful outcome meant that the band's future was saved.

Jagger and Richard arrived at the first day's hearing on June 27 in the guitarist's blue Bentley car. After the jury took just six minutes to find Mick Jagger guilty, he left in a gray van bound together with other prisoners to spend a night in Lewes Prison, Sussex. The following day, while Richard's case was being heard, Jagger was kept in a cell below the courtroom in case the trial ended that day.

While behind bars, he was visited by Marianne Faithfull, who brought him newspapers, fresh fruit, sixty tipped cigarettes, and a checkerboard. That same day, she was mentioned anonymously in court as the "girl in a fur-skin rug," who was "disclosing her nude body" and "apparently enjoy(ed) the situation."

On June 29, the pair were found guilty and sentenced—three months for Jagger, one year for Richard—drawing gasps from the public gallery. Jagger "swayed and almost collapsed," Richard was "white-faced but showed no emotion." The pair were driven away to prison, Mick to Brixton, Keith to Wormwood Scrubs, but the following day they were freed on appeal.

On July 1, *The Times* published an impassioned editorial, "Who Breaks a Butterfly on a Wheel?," which protested at the severity of the verdicts, and within a month, both sentences were lifted. "It felt lovely to be sure of freedom," said Jagger.

His Satanic Majesty meets His Holiness

"We are very happy. But we are trying to find even greater spiritual happiness to balance up our active lives."

Mick Jagger

above August 25, 1967: His Holiness the "Mystic from the Himalayas Maharishi Mahesh Yogi," flanked by an admiring follower and a bemused British Rail official. The Maharishi was on platform 13 at Euston Station in London, on his way to conduct a summer school in Bangor, north Wales.

IN THE AFTERMATH of Jagger and Richard's drug trials, there was a lot of soul-searching. In the press, it manifested itself in debates on the pop idols' responsibility to their fans, and the influence of pop culture on the nation's youth. Privately, the influence of drugs and the burden of responsibility prompted stars like Mick Jagger and the Beatles to ask deeper questions about themselves. It was a journey that would lead them to a diminutive long-haired mystic from India who called himself the Maharishi.

Described as "the world's leading expert on transcendental meditation," the Master —also known to his followers as His Holiness—had attracted the interest of the Beatles at a public lecture at the London Hilton Hotel on August 24. The group immediately canceled a recording session booked for the following day, and instead caught a train to Bangor, Wales, with the bearded Hindu sage. Mick Jagger and Marianne Faithfull, fast becoming England's

King and Queen of Flower Power, also joined the entourage.

Jagger's attendance at the Maharishi's weekend seminar was brief; on the Saturday, he had unexpectedly left a "think-in" meeting of meditators and was on his way back to London. He claimed he had to produce a recording session, and that because it wasn't with the Stones, he couldn't "get out of it." On the return journey, he attempted to explain why he made the trip: "I know he can teach me the direction in which I should go … I am just seek-

ing to be at one with the universe and myself—it's the same thing, really."

Insisting that the rest of the Stones were also interested in the teachings of the Maharishi, Jagger added: "We have pushed everything as far as we can by study and thought, but this is different. We are not doing it because we are unhappy. In fact, we are very happy. But we are trying to find even greater spiritual happiness to balance up our active lives. It will help us balance the material and spiritual sides of life in perfect happiness."

top July 8, 1967: While awaiting their appeal, Mick and Keith continued work on the next Stones album at Olympic Studios, in Barnes. Fans congregated outside hoping for a glimpse of pop's most notorious double act.

above Charlie Watts, untouched by voguish psychedelic fashions, strides across Church Road as he arrives for another session at Olympic. The Stones spent two weeks here in July trying to finish their sixth LP.

above After the late arrival of Beatle George Harrison had delayed the train's departure, the 3:05 from Euston eventually left the station with Mick Jagger and his incense-carrying girlfriend Marianne Faithfull sharing a carriage.

If the Stones' flirtation with Eastern enrichment was brief, their dalliance with social deviance was more enduring. At a press conference on July 31, after it had been announced that the pair's appeal against their court sentences had been successful, Mick Jagger faced many questions about his responsibility as a public figure.

One reporter raised the comment of Lord Parker, the Lord Chief Justice, who had told Jagger that as an idol to young people, he had "very grave responsibilities to them." The singer was asked how he proposed to exercise them. Jagger replied: "That's very difficult. One doesn't ask for responsibilities. I simply ask for my private life to be left alone. My responsibility is only to myself."

That evening, he took part in a special *World in Action* TV program that sought to discuss these matters in detail. Addressing a hastily assembled group that included William Rees-Mogg, editor of *The Times*, and members of the religious community, he said: "I am a rebel against society, but not an obvious one. People like me feel that things are wrong." He also claimed that "society has pushed me into this position of responsibility."

Later that night, at a party celebrating the two Stones' new-found freedom, Mick continued to flout convention by insisting he had no plans to marry. "Marianne is married and there is no question of a divorce, so we couldn't get married even if we wanted to. But we are not worried about that. Marriage doesn't interest us. We will probably buy a house—a big old one—and live together quite happily."

a dismal dull affair

"There's very few things in England that do transcend class."

Mick Jagger, *International Times*

August 13, 1967: Days after producing two songs for Marianne Faithfull at Decca's West Hampstead, London, studios, Mick and Marianne flew to Dublin for a weekend trip with their friend, Christopher Gibbs. While there, they dropped in, apparently uninvited, at the Butler Society Dinner, held in Kilkenny Castle. The pair, dressed in full hippie garb, clearly didn't fit in and after grabbing a bite to eat, made a hurried exit.

WHILE MICK JAGGER SOUGHT self-enlightenment, and in turn had tried to enlighten the establishment as a spokesman for youth, the rest of the band lay low. Brian Jones jetted in and out of Britain searching for that elusive few day's rest. "I just want to relax. It helps to ease the strain," he told reporters who'd flushed him out from his vacation hideaway in Marbella, Spain. Keith Richard flew out to Italy to spend time with girlfriend Anita Pallenberg, while Bill Wyman took the opportunity to do some production work with his protégés, the End. And Charlie? Well, he probably stayed at home with his wife Shirley.

When the Stones regrouped, early in September, they added finishing touches to their troubled *Satanic Majesties* album, before flying to New York for a special photographic session for the £25,000, three-dimensional LP cover. But first, there was the United States immigration authorities to contend with.

The four Stones, minus Mick Jagger but with photographer Michael Cooper in tow, had taken flight 707 from Heathrow on September 13. On arrival at Kennedy Airport, Keith Richard was taken to a

in another land

"Two Stones Barred by US: Jagger, Richard in Airport Drama"

Daily Mirror

facing page, main picture July 27, 1967: Brian Jones is shown the Who's public message of support for the Stones before jetting off for a vacation in Spain, with girlfriend Suki Poitier. "I haven't had a real holiday for a long time," he said.

facing page, far left Bound for New York: September 13, 1967. "The Stones, a motley group wearing a variety of fashions, caused heads to turn as they made their way through the Heathrow lounges out to flight 707." Photographer and friend Michael Cooper is pictured far left.

left October 29, 1967: Another trip to the Costa del Sol, another chance for Brian Jones, pictured here with Suki Poitier, to grab "a couple of days' rest." Hours after this shot was taken, he was back in London facing yet another drug charge.

below left October 8, 1967: The blessing of a new animal sanctuary near Chichester, Sussex. "Even if Rolling Stone Keith Richard was not at the service, his Great Dane puppy Winston still attracted a lot of reflected attention."

private room by immigration officers who questioned him for more than half an hour. Then they dropped a bombshell: He would be denied official entry into the United States. Allowed to spend the night in a New York hotel, the guitarist was required to attend a "deferred entry" examination at the immigration offices on Broadway the following morning.

When Mick Jagger arrived at the airport on a different flight (he'd caught an evening flight having returned to London from Paris with Marianne earlier in the day), he received exactly the same treatment. An immigration spokesman told reporters that a decision on whether the two Stones could enter the country would be made the next day, "in the light of information requested from London." It was obvious that news of the pair's drugs trial in Britain earlier that year had prompted the inquiry.

The story, which created headlines back in Britain, had blown over by the 15th. "Stones Can Stay in U.S." reported the *Daily Mirror* after Mick Jagger had called a friend in London with the news: "It's OK—we can all stay. The chap who gave us our visas even asked for an autograph." But immigration chiefs said they still wanted to study reports of the drug case in which the two Stones were involved, before deciding whether Jagger or Richard would be able to enter America again.

A S THE PRESSURES OF LIFE as a Rolling Stone intensified, the strain soon began to take its toll on Brian Jones. He'd formed the band (which he named after a Muddy Waters song) and had done most of the smart-talking in the early days as the group sought to bring R&B to a wider audience. Once that mission had been accomplished, Jones seemed to lose much of his drive and enthusiasm.

The only blond band member, it soon became obvious that it was more than his hair that made him stand out. As he'd mime to the group's songs on television, Jones would cast out knowing glances toward the camera. At the band's concerts, he'd be less concerned with hitting the right notes than in whipping the crowd into a frenzy. Picking up a variety of exotic instruments, such as the sitar, dulcimer, and marimbas, only served to emphasize his apartness.

Nudged down the band's hierarchy by the triumvirate of Jagger, Richard, and Andrew Oldham, and forced to endure Keith Richard's blossoming relationship with Anita Pallenberg, his one-time lover, Jones' tendency to rely on drink and drugs accelerated during 1967. To add to his woes, the authorities soon had him singled out as the most vulnerable Stone, and he became a regular target whenever an easy, morale-boosting drug bust was required.

Cruelly, the shadow of Jones' May 10 drug bust hung over him for almost six months. After court appearances in May and June, Brian, and his pal "Stash," were committed to trial on October 30. Stash was cleared; Jones was sentenced to nine months' jail after admitting charges of possessing cannabis and of allowing his flat to be used for drug-taking. Once again, it seemed that a Rolling Stone was being made a scapegoat, and in sentencing Jones, the judge told him: "You occupy a position by which you have a large following of youth and therefore it behoves you to set an example, and you have broken down on that." The prosecution accepted Jones' plea of not guilty to an additional charge of possessing cocaine and methedrine. He told the court: "I do smoke [hash]. But not cocaine, man. That is not my scene."

After a night in Wormwood Scrubs prison, Jones was released on October 31

it's so very lonely

pending an appeal. Stopping off at a pub on his way to a friend's house, Jones told reporters: "All I want is to be left alone". On November 12, the Appeal Court quashed his sentence and instead fined him £1,000, placed him on three years' probation and recommended medical treatment.

Three psychiatrists testified on his behalf, giving the public its first inkling that Jones was deeply troubled: Immature, emotionally unstable, and a man who might have committed suicide, were the verdicts.

The following day, the *Daily Mirror* devoted two full pages to a report headed

"Fame … has not so much gone to his head as imposed an additional strain upon an already fragile mental make-up."

Mr James Comyn, Brian Jones' counsel

"The Tormented Mind of Brian Jones." Jones was, said his lawyer, Mr. James Comyn, "a highly intelligent and extremely sensitive young man who had been catapulted to fame. This had not so much gone to his head as imposed an additional strain upon an already fragile mental makeup." Psychiatrist Dr. Walter Lindsey Neustatter described his interviews with the guitarist: "He came in most extraordinary clothes which one could only describe as flamboyant. I think he had gold trousers and something that looked like a fur rug." Despite this, Dr. Neustatter found the man inside the clothes quiet, thoughtful, and courteous.

In setting Jones' prison sentence aside, Lord Chief Justice Parker warned the Stone: "Remember, this is a degree of mercy which the court has shown. It is not a let-off. You cannot go boasting about saying you have been let off. If you … commit another offense of any sort, you will be brought back and punished for this offense. You know the sort of punishment you will get."

Jones' trial had additional ramifications in the Stones' camp. Mick's younger brother, Chris Jagger, was arrested and charged with abusive behavior and obstructing the police on October 30 during a "Free Brian Jones" protest march along the King's Road, Chelsea. On December 20, Chris, aged 19, was conditionally discharged for three years and ordered to pay ten guineas' costs.

facing page, far left June 2, 1967: Exotic Prince Stanislaus Klossowski, arrives at court to face drug charges with Jones, accompanied by someone who clearly wasn't a Rolling Stones fan.

facing page, center October 31, 1967: Brian Jones is whisked away in a Rolls-Royce having spent a night in Wormwood Scrubs prison after receiving a nine-month sentence for drug offenses. He was granted bail on appeal.

facing page, right June 2, 1967: A typically dapper Brian leaves a gaggle of girl fans speechless as he waltzes out of West London Magistrates Court after being bound over for trial in October.

far left Jones looks haunted and guilt-ridden as he sneaks into the central London Harley Street Nursing Home after narrowly avoiding a prison sentence. Days later, he was recuperating in the Priory Nursing Home, in Roehampton, south London.

left December 19, 1967: Mick's younger brother Chris, seen here with Caroline Coon, after being let out of jail on bail. The pair were arrested during a protest at the jail sentence of Brian Jones.

Chapter Four 1968
REGENERATION

THE EVENTS OF THE PAST TWELVE MONTHS had left the Rolling Stones drained and confused. Musically, they had reached a point whereby any additional experimentation would have sorely damaged their commercial viability. They were not in any shape to undergo morale-boosting concert tours. And now, with Andrew Oldham out of the picture, their manager was a New York accountant who had little understanding of the band's creative aspirations.

If 1967 had tested the Stones' ability to withstand intense public scrutiny, it had also forced them to reassess their roles as pop musicians. The articulate Mick Jagger, in particular, had—whether he liked it or not—become a "spokesman for his generation," and in turn, this new-found maturity was bound to be reflected in the band's music.

> ### "I am not the leader of the Rolling Stones. Charlie is the leader of the Rolling Stones."
> **Mick Jagger,** *Disc*

The lofty idealism that swept through youth culture during 1967 had begun to turn sour. The hippie dream of peace, love, and flowers had wilted. Instead, attentions turned from drug-induced fantasies to, in the United States, the reality of war in Vietnam and civil rights and, in Britain and mainland Europe, the class struggle. Impatient with the ways of the rules-obsessed, sexually repressed old order (which, judging by the letters pages in the popular press, preferred military service to soft drugs and nudity), teenagers stopped screaming at their idols and began to assert themselves politically, supporting strikes, attending marches, and organizing sit-ins. The moral authority of the establishment was questioned by a generation that regarded the British class system as outmoded. Inevitably the Rolling Stones, a most potent symbol of youth rebellion, got caught up in the cross fire.

In some ways, events had begun to overtake the Stones. Mick Jagger appeared on television to debate the present discontent with the establishment. The Stones wrote the definitive soundtrack to the spring student protests in "Street Fighting Man," with lyrics written after Jagger attended a demonstration in Grosvenor Square, London. But for much of 1968, the band retreated from the public's gaze, shunning the opportunity to become revolutionary Pied Pipers to concentrate on rescuing their musical career from the brink of disaster. Meanwhile, students and radicals were busy organizing themselves. ■

left November 29, 1968: The Rolling Stones at rehearsals for their performance on the *Frost on Saturday* show. It was Brian Jones' last television appearance with the band.

1968

"**Street Fighting Man**" starts life as "Did Everybody Pay Their Dues?," before becoming "Primo Grande (Street Fighting Man)." The song's backing track, featuring Keith Richard on acoustic guitar and Charlie Watts on a miniaturized toy drum-kit, is recorded on a cheap domestic cassette recorder, which the group build on in the studio.

It is announced students studying music at the University of California at Los Angeles will be required to study the Rolling Stones as part of the curriculum.

Early in 1968, the manufacturers of a new electronic instrument, the Moog synthesizer, send a demonstration model to Mick Jagger. He can be seen tinkering with it during his movie debut in *Performance*, shot in 1968, but not released until 1970.

During filming for Jean-Luc Godard's *One Plus One* movie, heat from the crew's lights set fire to the ceiling in Olympic Studios. While the rest of the group head for the exit, it was left to Bill Wyman and producer Jimmy Miller to salvage the master tapes.

The musicians in Jajouka show their appreciation of Brian Jones, to whom they still sing a tribute song: "Ah Brahim Jones/Jajouka Rolling Stone/Ah Brahim Jones/Jajouka really stoned."

Mick Jagger writes "Sympathy For The Devil" after reading Mikhail Bulgakov's novel, *The Master and Margarita*, in which Satan is implicated in the Russian Revolution. The song went through a variety of changes before arriving at the memorable fast, samba-beat arrangement.

Among the "obscenities" on the banned *Beggars Banquet* record sleeve are "God rolls his own!!," "Lyndon loves Mao," "Music from big brown," and "Wot no paper!"

According to the *Daily Mirror*, one of the guests at the society wedding between Lord Christopher Thynne and Miss Antonia Palmer, which took place on June 6, 1968, was "Mr. Michael Jagger, a vocalist with a popular string quartet, wearing a floppy hat and flowers."

premieres and performance

above January 28, 1968: A bearded Brian Jones with Diana Ross, Supremes' lead vocalist. The pair were pictured at a party held for the American singing group at the John Bulls restaurant in King's Road, Chelsea.

THE GREAT ROLLING STONES' fight-back, which brought them their first No. 1 single and critically acclaimed album in two years, was achieved on their own terms. After the disappointing sales of "We Love You" and the excesses of the *Satanic Majesties* album, they refused to be panicked back into the studio. Instead, they spent the best part of six months working on the *Beggars Banquet* LP, and were forced to wait while their record company, Decca, delayed its release because they objected to the graffitied lavatory wall sleeve. When the Stones weren't in the studio, they were often pursuing solo projects: Bill Wyman continued to produce the End; Brian Jones fulfilled his dream of recording some Moroccan mountain music; and Mick Jagger had finally done what the Stones had been threatening to do since 1964—launch into a movie career.

"Movies are kind of interesting. I'm going to learn a lot from movies."

Mick Jagger, *Los Angeles Free Press*

right January 18, 1968: Suki Poitier, by now Brian Jones' regular girlfriend, models "Maldwyn," a mauve, satin maxi blouse, in designer Ossie Clark's summer show. Another outfit was named after a Stones' song, "2,000 Light Years From Home."

far right During 1968, the public's fascination with Mick Jagger's romance with Marianne Faithfull intensified. Here they are pictured (from top) leaving Heathrow Airport for Dublin on April 13; arriving at the premiere of *2001: A Space Odyssey* on May1 ; and meeting Lord and Lady Montagu at the premiere of the musical *Hair* on December 4.

Movies had proved a notable money-spinner for Elvis Presley and Cliff Richard, and the success of the Beatles' *A Hard Day's Night* and *Help!* showed there was a healthy market for putting beat groups on the big screen, too. Encouraged by manager Andrew Oldham, the Stones had once obtained the rights to Anthony Burgess' novel *A Clockwork Orange*, which chimed perfectly with their bad-boy image. The British censors clearly weren't happy and the project was quietly abandoned. Another idea, a screen version of Dave Willis' *Only Lovers Left Alive* got as far as a finished script, but it too was canceled. Likewise *Back, Behind and in Front*, a proposed Andrew Oldham/Allen Klein production featuring a Jagger/Richard score, which was scheduled to begin shooting in April 1966.

The Stones only had Peter Whitehead's rarely seen tour documentary, *Charlie Is My Darling*, and a handful of songs in the American concert flick, *Teenage Command Performance*, to show for their endeavors. That changed during 1968, when two notable projects came their way. Jean-Luc Godard, the *enfant terrible* of the French new wave, signed the band up for *One Plus One*, a tangle of politics, both revolutionary and cultural, for which the Stones were filmed working on a new song, "Sympathy For The Devil," at Olympic Studios.

Even more notable was *Performance*, a major Warner Bros production codirected by maverick talents Donald Cammell and Nic Roeg. Although Jagger signed the deal in May, filming didn't begin until the fall, conveniently allowing the Stones time to finish work on their album. A dark distillation of late-sixties bohemia and the criminal underworld, *Performance*—for which Jagger dyed his hair and appeared naked alongside costar Anita Pallenberg—is now regarded by some as one of the finest British films ever made.

Movies were also important to the Stones in a more direct way during 1968. Although the band had been making promotional shorts for several singles since 1966, Michael Lindsay-Hogg's movie for "Jumpin' Jack Flash," the Stones' first single in nine months, was notable in that this relatively straight clip of the group performing the song (albeit heavily madeup) was seized upon by television stations around the world—thus saving the Stones the effort of traveling to far-flung places to promote it. They were rewarded with their first British

No. 1 since "Paint It Black" in 1966.

This gave the band more time to themselves, which helps explain why Mick Jagger and Brian Jones in particular could be found at a variety of social events during the year. At a party held in honor of American singing group the Supremes, Jones rubbed shoulders with songwriter Lionel Bart, singer Tom Jones, actresses Lynn and Vanessa Redgrave, and actor Michael Caine. And revealingly, while his attendance at Rolling Stones recording sessions was erratic, Brian often dropped by at Olympic when Jimi Hendrix was there. But his main concern was bringing the music of the Master Musicians of Jajouka to the public's attention, and in August he traveled to Morocco to record a fascinating performance of ritual ceremonial music. It was later released on LP.

above May 12, 1968: The Stones made an unexpected appearance at the annual *New Musical Express* Poll Winners' Concert, which took place at the Empire Pool, Wembley. It was their first British concert for 18 months.

right The band looked in better spirits than they'd done for some time, and received an ecstatic reception from the crowd after playing their latest 45, "Jumpin' Jack Flash," and "(I Can't Get No) Satisfaction."

far right The Stones pictured in their dressing room with the trophy for Best R&B Group. It was the fifth consecutive year they'd won the award, but it was to be their last—the annual show was canceled after 1968.

facing page, top right Marianne Faithfull, flanked by Anita Pallenberg (in fringed jacket), throws a bunch of red roses toward the stage. Jagger responded by hurling one of his shoes into the audience.

"It was just like old times. In fact, it was better than old times. One of the best receptions we have ever had. We were all delighted."

Mick Jagger, *New Musical Express*

a quick

flash

GUILTY

ON MAY 2, 1968, Brian Jones moved into a new flat at Royal Avenue House, King's Road, in Chelsea. He'd barely had time to settle in before the police were on his back again. At 7.20 A.M. on May 21, four of them forced their way in with a warrant, and after a search, confronted the weary Stone with a ball of yarn in which was concealed, they said, a lump of cannabis. Jones was taken to the local police station, charged with possession of the drug, and appeared later that day at Marlborough Street Magistrates Court, where he was released for three weeks on £2,000 bail. Jones went straight from the court to spend

above September 26, 1968: A Stone under pressure. Brian waits for lunch at the Ship pub in a break from his case at Inner London Sessions. Girlfriend Suki Poitier and chauffeur Tom Keylock appear surprisingly relaxed.

a few days at the Priory Nursing Home in Roehampton, a south London suburb. Weeks later, on July 11, as teenage fans sobbed outside the court, he was bound over for trial.

The bust took its toll. Jones, already worn down by the events of the previous year, became increasingly ostracized from the rest of the group, who were busy picking up the pieces of their fragmented career. Brian Jones was in no shape to contribute. He frequently collapsed from fatigue midway through recording sessions, and when he did manage to stay awake, his contributions were often ignored. With the availability of session musicians like pianist Nicky Hopkins and slide guitarist Ry Cooder, the Stones were able to manage without their erstwhile leader.

The threat of imprisonment hung over Brian Jones throughout the summer, so as the jury at Inner London Sessions found him guilty when the case came to trial, on September 26, everyone feared the worst. The situation was so grave that even Mick Jagger and Keith Richard turned up at the court in time to hear the "guilty" verdict. But, thankfully, it was Jones' persecution complex that received a knock that day. Instead of imposing a prison sentence, the court chairman, Mr. S. E. Seaton, chose, instead, to fine Jones £50 and issue him with another grave warning: "You must keep clear of this stuff … For goodness' sake, don't get into trouble again. If you do, there will be real trouble." But Brian still protested his innocence: "I had no idea the cannabis resin was in the ball of wool. I didn't even know the wool was there.

"When the jury announced the guilty verdict," said Jones afterward, "I was sure I was going to jail for at least a year. It was such a wonderful relief when I heard I was only going to be fined. I'm happy to be free. It's wonderful." Mick Jagger added: "We are very pleased that Brian didn't have to go to jail. Money doesn't matter."

"I knew I was innocent, but everything seems to happen to me."

Brian Jones, *Daily Mirror*

above right Jones makes his way to Inner London Sessions, flanked by Suki and Tom.

above far right Brian gets out of his car to face the jury. When police arrived to search his flat, he was alleged to have told them: "Why do you have to pick on me?"

right It's great to be free! Jones receives some much-needed support from Mick and Keith after narrowly avoiding a jail sentence. "I was sure I was going to jail for at least a year," he told reporters.

Frost and the Devil

"We have become very interested in magic, and we are very serious about this ... "

Keith Richard, *Sunday Express*

this page The group made their first public appearance for six months as guests on the *Frost on Saturday* TV show, broadcast on November 30, 1968. These pictures were shot during rehearsals the previous day.

facing page A few weeks earlier, on October 12, Mick had starred in the first episode of the show discussing sex before marriage with the scourge of the permissive society, Mrs. Mary Whitehouse. The debate had been prompted by the announcement of Marianne Faithfull's pregnancy—despite the fact that she was still married to another man, John Dunbar.

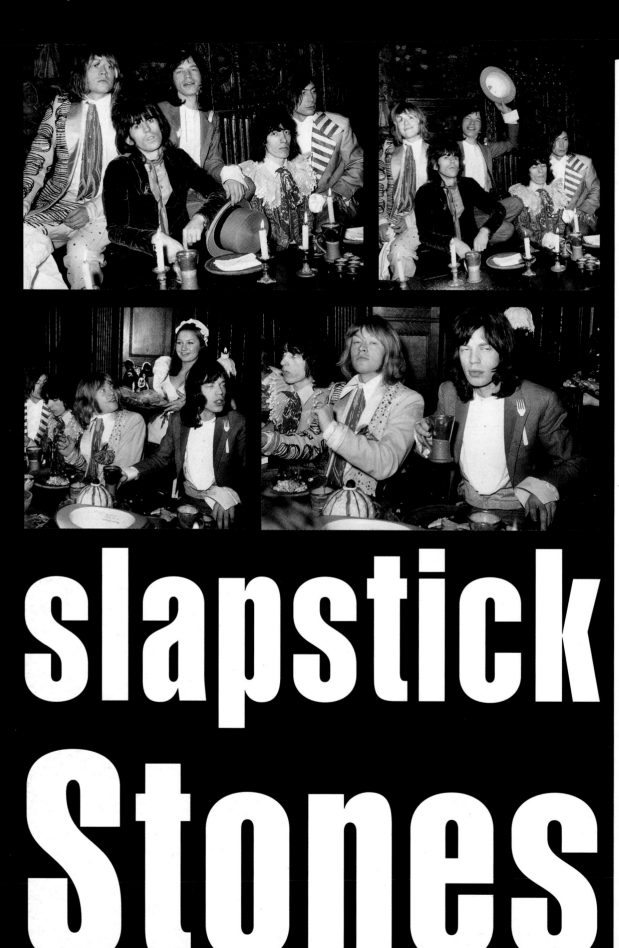

slapstick Stones

THE ROLLING STONES LAUNCHED their long-awaited *Beggars Banquet* LP with a medieval-style party at the Kensington Gore Hotel, London, on December 5, 1968. The event ended in true slapstick style—with guests being pelted with custard pies. But making the record had been a serious business.

The band knew that their previous album, *Their Satanic Majesties Request*, for all its wayward glory, had shocked fans. They had also seen that other major acts, notably the Beatles and Bob Dylan, had begun to shun the psychedelic excesses of the previous year and switched to an earthier, back-to-basics sound. Suitably inspired, the group emerged at the end of the year with *Beggars Banquet*, undoubtedly their most complete album yet.

Gone was the excess of studio-enhanced, psychedelic effects. Gone, too, were the undisciplined, aimless jams made up on the spot during recording sessions. This time, the group had approached the album methodically, first road-testing Jagger and Richard's new songs in low-key sessions at home or in rehearsal studios. When the group (Brian excepted) knew what they were doing, the Stones then joined up-and-coming record producer Jimmy Miller at Olympic. This long-winded process yielded immediate and long-term results—*Beggars Banquet* won rave reviews at the time, and is now regarded as one of the key Rolling Stones albums.

Unlike *Satanic Majesties*, *Beggars Banquet* was crammed full of classic songs. From the dark and teasing opening cut, "Sympathy For The Devil," to the insurrectionary and subversive "Street Fighting Man," the album had set the group up for what was to become the most artistically satisfying few years in their career.

facing page The Stones launch their long-awaited *Beggars Banquet* LP with a press party at the Kensington Gore Hotel's Elizabethan Room. The original idea was to hire a room in the Tower of London. In keeping with the theme of the record, the party was designed along the lines of a medieval banquet, with waitresses dressed as serving wenches and a boar's head soaked in red wine as the centerpiece of the seven-course feast.

"They threw a lunch party to launch their new record and then threw custard pies for the sheer pleasure of doing it."

Daily Mirror

above Bill Wyman hides his face as the band's PR man Les Perrin takes aim with "a pie oozing with a meringue mixture." The Stones had succumbed to "the oldest gag in the book—custard-pie throwing," sniffed the *Daily Mail*.

left Mick Jagger's pie-in-the-face for Brian Jones provided the cue for an all-out food fight. Even guest of honor Lord Harlech, earlier described by Mick as "a groove, a lovely cat," needed his suit dry-cleaned afterward.

roll up, roll up

THE *ROLLING STONES' Rock 'n' Roll Circus*, an all-star extravaganza filmed for television in December 1968, was the band's answer to the Beatles' ambitious, psychedelic-era project *Magical Mystery Tour*. But because this was 1968 and not 1967, the emphasis had now reverted back to entertainment, albeit of a vaguely surreal style, rather than baffling the audience with nonsensical action and unfathomable story lines, as the Beatles had done.

"You've heard of Oxford Circus, you've heard of Piccadilly Circus, and this is the Rolling Stones' Rock 'n' Roll Circus."

Mick Jagger

The idea was simple: Assemble a cast of rock 'n' roll luminaries, add a variety of circus acts and an audience, invite them to a television studio designed to resemble a traveling circus, and let the cameras roll. That was the easy part: the three days' filming, over December 10, 11, and 12, might have been exhausting, but director Michael Lindsay-Hogg (who'd known the Stones since his days directing *Ready, Steady, Go!*) had more than enough material for what was intended as a one-hour television show. The *Daily Mirror* reported on December 12 that "The Stones have laid out £50,000 on the show, which they will sell to the highest bidder for screening in the New Year." But for various reasons, not least the fact that the band felt they'd been below-par for their own performance, filmed during the early hours of December 12, the *Rolling Stones' Rock 'n' Roll Circus* languished in a vault until 1995, when it was reedited for video and CD release.

The project was conceived by Mick Jagger in mid-November 1968, shortly after he'd finished work on his first movie role, playing the faded rock star Turner in *Performance*. By this time, the demarcation lines between pop and established arts like movies and photography were becoming blurred, and Jagger seized on *Rock 'n' Roll Circus* as an opportunity to widen his creative orbit. The event also indicated that the Stones weren't prepared to return to the punishing single/tour/album schedule

that had dominated their career up until spring of that year.

A variety of acts were quickly recruited. The Who were the first to come on board, although plans to add the Steve Winwood-fronted band, Traffic, failed to materialize. Country star Johnny Cash couldn't make it, but American blues performer Taj Mahal could. Jagger and his fellow organizers sifted through a pile of tapes of up-and-coming homegrown bands, and decided Jethro Tull were a better bet than Led Zeppelin (even though both Jimmy Page and John Paul Jones had previously worked with the Stones as session musicians). Naturally Marianne Faithfull wasn't difficult to book, but Brigitte Bardot (intended as the show's ringmistress) and Mia Farrow proved more elusive.

The final masterstroke was tempting a Beatle to turn up. Better still, John Lennon brought along guitarist Eric Clapton, and with Mitch Mitchell, drummer for the Jimi Hendrix Experience, and the Stones' Keith Richard (who switched to bass) in tow, they formed what the press called "a supergroup" for the occasion.

With all the acts in place, the Intertel Studios, Wembley, were booked for three days, between December 10 and 12, 1968, and after a first day given over to rehearsals, filming began on the 11th. In the absence of Bardot as compere, Mick Jagger stepped in as ringmaster and got the show underway with the words: "You've heard of Oxford Circus, you've heard of Piccadilly Circus, and this is the Rolling Stones' Rock 'n' Roll Circus."

After several of the other acts had filmed their performances, the supergroup, now billed as the Dirty Mac, took to the stage for a version of Lennon's "Yer Blues." Then Yoko Ono joined them and proceeded to emit a string of high-pitched wailing noises over a loose jam, subsequently titled "Whole Lotta Yoko."

By the time the Stones walked on, it was 2 A.M. on December 12. When they had finished three hours later, they'd filmed "Jumpin' Jack Flash," three songs from the just-issued *Beggars Banquet* ("Parachute Woman," "Sympathy For The Devil," and "Salt Of The Earth"), and premiered one new number, "You Can't Always Get What You Want." As the subsequent video release shows, it was a performance to be proud of—but it was to be their last appearance on stage with Brian Jones.

facing page John Lennon and girlfriend Yoko Ono were among the guest celebrities at the *Rolling Stones' Rock 'n' Roll Circus*, television spectacular. But the show was later scrapped because the Stones were unhappy with the finished product.

right Brian Jones was subdued at the *Circus*, his final public appearance with the Rolling Stones. He seemed more concerned with entertaining model Donyale Luna, who played the part of the fire-eater's assistant in the show.

Chapter Five 1969
SIXTIES FAREWELL

A PERIOD OF RELATIVE STABILITY DURING 1968 had given the Rolling Stones time to consider where their career was going. The results had already begun to bear fruit, with the success of "Jumpin' Jack Flash" and *Beggars Banquet*. With more hit records, and the band's first concert tour since spring 1967, that stability continued throughout 1969. But there was still some unfinished business to attend to, and some uncomfortable twists in the tale.

Being a pop star had clearly changed since the carefree days of 1964. The Stones no longer had a hands-on manager pressurizing them into completing more records and more tours. Instead, they were increasingly taking control over their destiny. They chose when and where to record, and who with; they even had a say in when to release their records. During 1968, their output had shrunk to just one single and one album, setting in motion a regime that the band loosely adhered to for the next decade.

> "Mick Jagger, fast emerging as the group's keenest businessman, was one of the key spokesmen of his generation."

A degree of stability had also entered the Stones' world. They'd become property-owning celebrities with their own households to maintain. Rock music had become an increasingly lucrative business, and inevitably the group sought to protect their interests—and their privacy. Mick Jagger was fast emerging as the group's keenest businessman, although that didn't harm his stature as one of the key spokesmen of his generation, alongside John Lennon, Bob Dylan, and Pete Townshend of the Who.

Not everyone managed to traverse the 1967 watershed with such ease as the Stones. The Beatles and Cilla Black aside, the stars of Merseybeat had been quickly forgotten. Yet, the group's musical reputation, which had nosedived (at least commercially) during 1967, made a miraculous recovery towards the end of the decade.

There was only one exception to the Stones' new-found enthusiasm: Brian Jones—a problem which would resolve itself in the most tragic circumstances during 1969. ■

left Death of a Rolling Stone. Four weeks after leaving the band, Brian Jones drowned in his own swimming pool. It has since been claimed that the verdict of death by misadventure should have been one of manslaughter—or even murder.

1969

In May, it was reported that the Rolling Stones would be launching their own record label, Pear, a move inspired by the Beatles' Apple Records.

News of Brian Jones' death filtered through to Olympic Studios when the Stones were working on a version of Stevie Wonder's "I Don't Know Why." The song wasn't released until 1975.

Brian Jones wrote his own epitaph in a telegram sent to his parents following a drug bust: "Please don't judge me too harshly." The Stones paid tribute to him on the cover of their *Through The Past Darkly (Big Hits Vol. 2)* sleeve: "With this you see, remember me/And bear me in your mind/Let all the world say what they may/Speak of me as you find."

Having worn his Greek-inspired Mr. Fish "dress" to an all-white ball earlier in the week, Mick Jagger had designer Ossie Clark run him up a snakeskin suit for the Stones' Hyde Park appearance. But the hot weather forced him to break with showbiz convention and he reverted back to his party dress for the gig.

Despite Mick Jagger being a major shareholder, the launch of a British edition of the San Francisco-based *Rolling Stone* magazine proved unsuccessful, and the London operation was forced to close in November.

When asked how "satisfied" he was during a press conference for the American tour, Mick Jagger replied: "Financially satisfied, sexually satisfied, emotionally trying."

The 1969 American tour yields one of the first bootleg records, *Liver Than You'll Ever Be*. Sales were so impressive the Stones were forced to counter with their own official document of the tour, *Get Yer Ya-Ya's Out!*

A little-known movie, *Michael Kohlhaas*, starring Anita Pallenberg and Anna Karina, is released in November and finds Keith Richard making a cameo appearance. Keith sacrificed two inches of hair to make his movie debut.

Mick's Honky Tonk woman

left May 6, 1969: Marsha Hunt, star of the hippie stageshow *Hair*, prepares to launch her singing career with "Walk On Gilded Splinters." The striking American had just begun a relationship with Mick Jagger.

ON NOVEMBER 20, 1968, it was announced that Marianne Faithfull, then five-and-a-half months into her pregnancy, had lost her baby. The tragedy proved to be a major turning point in her relationship with Mick Jagger. While the singer plowed himself into work, Marianne turned to hard drugs to numb the emotional pain.

On the surface, all seemed well. The pair had taken an extended Christmas holiday to South America with Keith Richard and Anita Pallenberg, themselves expecting their first child. On their return, they decorated their Cheyne Walk house in London with oriental carpets and crystal chandeliers. Then, in February 1969, Marianne released her first single in two years only to see it withdrawn just days later. The song, a harrowing tale titled "Sister Morphine," was too much for the suits at Decca. Another lifeline for Marianne—the resurrection of her singing career—had been cut off.

Another drug bust, at Cheyne Walk on May 28, added to the couple's woes. While Detective Sergeant Robin Constable talked to Mick and Marianne, his uniformed colleagues searched the premises. After being charged with cannabis possession, Jagger, dressed in a pink velvet suit, returned home looking tired. "Six or seven of them arrived just after Marianne and I had finished our tea," he explained to reporters unhelpfully.

Then there was Marsha Hunt. Shortly after Marianne had miscarried, the couple had attended the premiere of a controversial new London musical, *Hair*. The production, which brought a little hippie philosophy to the West End stage, created headlines—not least because the cast briefly appeared naked on stage. Among its bevy of rising stars was Marsha Hunt—black, beautiful, and intelligent—an American performer living in London.

Marsha was also talented and ambitious. Early in 1969, she'd been given a record deal by Track Records, then enjoying much success with the Jimi Hendrix Experience, the Who, and the Crazy World of Arthur Brown. She had a brief liaison with the then little-known Marc Bolan, before gaining notoriety by inadvertently exposing her breasts on the TV-show *Top of the Pops* while

"Brian Jones quits the Stones as group clash over songs."

Daily Sketch

performing her first single, "Walk On Gilded Splinters."

Inevitably, Marsha Hunt had aroused Jagger's attentions, too. He asked her whether she'd pose with the band for the cover of the Stones' forthcoming single, "Honky Tonk Women." With her own career taking off, she declined the offer, but that didn't stop Jagger from paying her a late-night visit at her flat in Endsleigh Court in Bloomsbury. He stayed until dawn—thus marking the beginning of a secret, year-long relationship that would result in Jagger's first acknowledged love-child.

Musically, the Stones were back on the right path—with the exception of Brian Jones, whose contributions had by now

dwindled to almost nothing. When the group returned to the studio in February 1969, to begin work on a follow-up to the *Beggars Banquet* LP, they were joined by session musicians including Ry Cooder and Nicky Hopkins. Brian, attempting to get himself together in his new country house, was rarely around. A decision on Jones' future within the band was imminent, its outcome increasingly inevitable.

On May 30, the Stones regrouped at Olympic Studios, in Barnes, to record a new single. Only this time, they were joined by Mick Taylor, a shy young guitarist best known for his work as part of veteran blues man John Mayall's Bluesbreakers, where he'd followed in the footsteps of Eric Clapton and Fleetwood Mac's Peter Green. The sessions that weekend proved remarkably successful. The following weekend, Mick Jagger, Keith Richard, and Charlie Watts drove down to Jones' Sussex house to

break the news. They had found a replacement for him; Brian Jones was no longer a Rolling Stone. Jones was hardly surprised, and while outwardly philosophical, deep down he was heartbroken. After a generous financial settlement had been agreed, his old pals drove off in the knowledge that they'd secured a new future for themselves.

That evening, on June 8, 1969, a press release was hastily issued. Brian was quoted as saying: "The Rolling Stones music is not to my taste any more … I no longer see eye to eye with the others over the discs we are cutting." Jagger added that: "The only solution to our problem was for Brian to leave us … We've parted on the best of terms."

Mick Taylor officially joined the Rolling Stones at an afternoon press conference in London's Hyde Park on June 13. Mick Jagger told reporters: "He doesn't play anything like Brian. He's a blues player and wants to play rock 'n' roll, so that's OK."

above June 13, 1969: The Rolling Stones unveil Mick Taylor, their replacement for Brian Jones, at a press conference in London's Hyde Park. "He's very level-headed," said Mick Jagger. "I don't think we'll have any trouble."

strip, bottom May 29, 1969: Mick and Marianne leave Marlborough Street Magistrates Court after being charged with possessing cannabis, following a raid on their home the previous evening.

strip, top three The pair were back in court just weeks later, on June 23, when they were each remanded on £50 bail. Minder Tom Keylock (top, center) keeps the waiting crowds at bay.

tragedy at the farm

TO THOSE WHO KNEW HIM BEST, "Brian Jones of the Stones Found Dead" was a newspaper headline waiting to happen. But the rest of the world was shocked by the news of his death at 27 when they woke up on July 3, 1969.

In the *Daily Mirror*'s 3:30 A.M. edition, reporter Don Short wrote that the Stones' tour manager Tom Keylock first warned him that there had been "trouble" at Brian's house. Keylock had tried calling the Stone but got no reply. Short passed on the grim news: "This is a terrible shock," said Keylock. "I spoke to Brian yesterday morning and he was full of spirits and raring to go."

The following day, attention focused on Anna Wohlin, Brian Jones' latest girlfriend, who had left Jones swimming in his pool for a few minutes and returned to find him lying unconscious in the water. As the 22-year-old Swedish student went into hiding, the press began to speculate that the late Stone had probably died after an asthma attack.

Don Short penned a touching tribute to Jones under the headline: "The Wild Pooh of Pooh Corner." "Throughout his career he was cast in the eternal role of the rebel— the wild man in a wild business. But, in his own language, it wasn't his scene." Short described Jones as "an intense introvert— far removed from the rebel we knew." He also referred to Brian's disappointment that the songwriting team of Jagger and Richard had determined in which direction the Stones' music would go. "It's not that I dislike their music," Jones had told him. "It's great, but there must be a fair crack of the whip. As a group, we've got to consider all channels of music, mine included."

The reporter turned to Pat Andrews, the mother of one of Jones' sons, in a bid to discover why there had been so many girls in his life. "He had to have girls around him because of his insecurity," she told him, adding that "he had to prove his male instincts." More revealingly, she said: "He was the hardest boy in the world to understand and I think we all believed we could understand him if we tried long enough ... But really no one ever could."

That weekend, the *Sunday Mirror* ran an editorial contrasting the fortunes of "The Jones Boy and the Jones Girl." Tennis star Ann Jones had just won the ladies' singles title at Wimbledon. She was a forceful individual who had succeeded in her "battle for survival." Ann Jones had the world at her feet. For Brian Jones, "a kind of social Houdini, a wild spirit who could laugh at rules and taboos whether they concerned drugs or morality," the world was at an end. "For the Jones Girl the laurels. For the Jones Boy the wreath."

On July 6, when the papers were full of pictures of fans enjoying the sun at the

The inquest into Jones' death on July 7 was something of a relief from all the speculation, although the headlines the following morning—"Drinks and Drugs Killed Brian Jones"—sprang no real surprises. A nurse, Janet Lawson, who had been at the house on the evening of Jones' death, told the coroner that Brian "was a bit unsteady on his feet" after drinking spirits with his girlfriend Anna Wohlin. Then, against Lawson's advice, he went for a swim with Lawson's partner, Frank Thorogood, who'd been working on Jones' farmhouse for many weeks. She left the swimming pool to go inside the house, but returned to see

main picture Jones' six-bedroom country retreat in Hartfield, Sussex, once belonged to Winnie the Pooh author, A. A. Milne. A life-size statue of the author's son, Christopher Robin, can be seen in the foreground.

above Tom Keylock, the Stones' road manager, talks to reporters outside Cotchford Farm the day after Jones' death.

top left Builder Frank Thorogood comforts Jones' girlfriend, Anna Wohlin, as they arrive for the inquest at East Grinstead. Both were with Jones on the night he died.

below, far left July 3, 1969: Pat Andrews, 24, with her seven-year-old son by Brian Jones, Mark. "All we have received is 50 shillings a week from Brian," she told reporters. "We are having to live in a London hostel because we have no other money."

left Another former girlfriend reported to be pressing a claim on Jones' estate is Linda Lawrence, who flew in from Hollywood with her son by Brian Jones, five-year-old Julian. She had received a £1,000 lump sum settlement.

below Brian Jones' six-month-old Afghan hound, Rufus. Jones also had a spaniel named Emily. Unfortunately, the company he kept wasn't always so devoted to his well-being, especially on the night of his death.

> ## "I can't say what his plans were. But he was full of enthusiasm for them."
>
> **Tom Keylock,** *Daily Mirror*

Stones' Hyde Park concert, an old friend from Jones' hometown of Cheltenham, Dick Hattrell, claimed: "He was on the down road. There was always a sense of doom about him." Hattrell also insisted that Jones had clear plans for his future away from the Stones, stating that his ambition had been "to revert to pure blues music, to gather round him the finest blues musicians and form a new group." But he added that Jones would have lived only a matter of weeks had he not quickly found his potential.

him lying at the bottom of the pool.

Pathologist Albert Sachs added that Jones was in extremely poor health. The musician's liver was twice the normal weight and in an advanced state of fatty degeneration, and his heart was fat and flabby. But none of this has ever satisfied rumormongers and conspiracy theorists, and three books have since claimed that Jones died under circumstances that were probably closer to manslaughter, or perhaps even murder.

butterflies

in the sun

"Brian would have wanted it to go on. We will now do the concert for him."
Mick Jagger

facing page, far left July 5, 1969: The Stones arrive for the Hyde Park concert, the band's first real London show since September 1966. Behind Mick Jagger is new guitarist 21-year-old Mick Taylor, making his Stones debut.

facing page, top left Mick Jagger, attired in a fetching Mr. Fish dress, precedes the Stones' performance by reading a Shelley poem, "Adonais," as a tribute to Brian Jones.

THE JULY 5 CONCERT in Hyde Park, which took place just forty-eight hours after the death of Brian Jones, proved to be the most traumatic in the band's career to date.

While the show had been planned for several weeks, Jones' death guaranteed the event was hastily billed by the Stones as a tribute to their late guitarist. Mick Jagger, who wore a white Mr. Fish dress, preceded the Stones' performance by reading some lines from Shelley's "Adonais" poem, penned as an elegy to the poet Keats. A period of relative silence ensued while he spoke: "Peace! Peace! He is not dead. He hath awaken from the dream of life … "

After Jagger finished his tribute, 2,000 white butterflies were released, and the Stones got the show underway with a rarely played blues number, "I'm Yours, She's Mine." The overall performance was ragged, as one might have expected, given the shock of Jones' death. Matters weren't helped by the fact that new guitarist Mick Taylor was making his debut in front of more than 250,000 people.

Although the biggest open-air rock event of its kind, the concert in Hyde Park sat awkwardly with the love 'n' peace ambience. It was free, but with leather-clad Hell's Angels policing the event, and Jones' death uppermost in people's minds, the bright summer's day was tainted by darker emotions. Worse was to come.

In December, another open-air, free concert, at the Altamont Speedway track, California, ended with the gruesome death of a spectator. Once again, Hell's Angels had been recruited to provide security for the show, but on this occasion, the combination of bad acid, too much beer, and, some whispered, the Stones' messianic vibe, sent the event spiraling into chaos.

frock 'n' roll

above Among those getting a stage-eye view were Marianne Faithfull (face hidden) with her son Nicholas, manager Allen Klein, MC Sam Cutler (in dark glasses), and sixth Stone Ian Stewart, nursing a bottle of beer.

right Marianne and Nicholas backstage. Jones' death hit her particularly hard, and probably hastened her descent into heroin addiction.

"It was a show that ended in hysteria, with a young girl being carried off screaming after trying to throw herself at Jagger."

Sunday Mirror

KODAK SAFETY FILM   KOD

5A   6   6A   7   7A   8   8A

KODAK SAFETY FILM   KOD

5A   6   6A   7   7A   8   8A

above and left Hell's Angels guard the VIP area in what was generally a trouble-free day. The same could not be said about a Stones concert at Altamont, California, in December, when the motorcycle fanatics were responsible for the death of a fan.

above and right July 10, 1969: A crowd of around 500 people lined Hatherly Road as the funeral procession made its way to the cemetery from 900-year-old St. Mary's Church in Cheltenham, where Brian Jones used to sing as a young choirboy.

far right A floral tribute depicting the "Gates of Heaven" from the Rolling Stones, and a guitar-shaped wreath from Brian's parents and his sister Barbara, lay in the Jones' drive before the service.

"Brian had little patience with authority, convention, and tradition."

Canon Hugh Evan Hopkins

far left Charlie Watts and his wife Shirley, having just heard the rector speak of Jones' rebelliousness: "He was typical of many of his generation who have come to see in the Rolling Stones an expression of their whole attitude to life."

left Bill Wyman, with his girlfriend Astrid Lundström, and Charlie Watts on their way to the graveside. They were the only Stones to attend the ceremony. Frank Thorogood, who was with Jones when he died, is seen in the foreground (right).

paint it black

left Dozens of girls, many dressed in black and clutching red roses, had converged on the spa town in Gloucestershire. As the bronze casket was lowered into the grave, many tossed their roses in after it.

Jagger down under

facing page With newly-shorn hair and a ragged beard, Mick Jagger—as Australia's legendary outlaw Ned Kelly—looks on as the crew prepares to shoot the next scene.

WITH HIS FIRST MOVIE, *Performance*, yet to hit the screens, Mick Jagger arrived in Sydney, Australia, on July 8, 1969 to begin shooting a second movie. He'd been cast in the lead role of *Ned Kelly*, Tony Richardson's movie about Australia's favorite folk hero. But if he thought he was leaving his worries back in Britain, he was wrong.

As soon as Mick and Marianne Faithfull (who had been cast as Ned Kelly's sister)

"I won't see the movie when it's finished. Once I've finished doing something that's the end of it for me. I never go back."

Mick Jagger

touched down, they were shadowed by security guards hired to protect them from the "Glenrowan Gang," who'd made threats to kidnap the star and cut off all his hair. (The real Ned Kelly was captured after a gun battle with police at Glenrowan, Victoria.) Local newspapers stoked up the country's dissatisfaction at a long-haired Englishman portraying Australia's notorious bushranger: "My first numbing impression when I saw him was, 'This isn't Mick Jagger. It's Barry Humphries having us on,' " noted one commentator.

The controversy was soon forgotten. Shortly after arriving in the country, Marianne Faithfull was rushed from the couple's thirteenth-floor hotel suite to St. Vincent's Hospital in Sydney. Despite claims by Jagger at the time that his girlfriend was "suffering from extreme exhaustion," it soon transpired she had entered a life-threatening coma after a suicide attempt. In the days that followed, as Marianne lay comatose, Jagger was forced to stick to his filming schedule, flying back to Sydney from Melbourne at every opportunity to be by her bedside.

On July 13, Marianne finally opened her eyes and, seeing Jagger, murmured a brief "Hello." After a period of recuperation at a private psychiatric ward, on August 6, she was well enough to fly to Melbourne and spend a week with Jagger before returning home to Britain. "I was virtually dead,"

right, top two pictures Having an Englishman play Ned Kelly aroused Aussie passions, but one crew member insisted: "He's the most sincere and likeable star who's come to this country."

below right Between takes, Mick Jagger shares a coach with Australian actor Ronald Golding. The newspapers, filled with stories about Marianne's suicide bid or Jagger's unsuitability for the movie role, wouldn't have made relaxing reading.

below far right Jagger talks to Constable Harold Oxley, a member of the New South Wales Police Force, who is assigned to the movie set while shooting takes place in the township of Bungendore.

she told reporters. "They saved my life."

The next shock came when photographs of Mick as Ned Kelly began to appear in the press early in August. "Gone are the flowing locks and pouting lips the Rolling Stones fans know," commented the *Daily Mirror*. Gone, too, would have been Jagger himself had a shooting accident on August 19 been any more serious. Instead, the stray bullet from the pistol he had been holding fired agonizingly into his hand.

The four-month filming had given Jagger time to reflect on recent events, and he spoke exclusively to the *Daily Mirror* from the location set of *Ned Kelly*, thirty-eight miles south of Canberra. "This is the first big challenge I've ever had as an actor," he told Patrick McCarville, actor, writer, and his dialogue coach. "I've got to live the part if I'm to get the best of me." That included, he said, going for days without washing, to recreate the authentic stench of an unwashed nineteenth-century outlaw.

During his time down under he learned about British imperialism, which he contrasted with his own treatment in England. "At home we couldn't walk down the street and say 'bum' without getting arrested. But in our colonies we plundered, murdered,

raped, thieved, and generally ravaged every black, brown, or yellow poor chump unfortunate enough to be 'discovered' by us."

There was also plenty of time for fun off the set. Near the end of the filming, horse-minder Jack Buraston decided to throw a party in Mick's honor. "It'll only be a quiet little do," he assured the star. On the night, 500 people turned up, most of them gatecrashers. When Mick arrived, everyone seemed to be fighting, so "he took one step from his car, looked around—got back in his car and drove home."

Mick didn't always find the Aussie hospitality so unwelcoming. "These Australian women amaze me," he said. "The Aussie birds look fantastic in bikinis. Sexiest things you'll see anywhere in the world. They've got this sexy bronzed skin and their bodies are fantastic." But on the set, far away from the exotic sights of Sydney Harbour, it was a different story. "Jesus," said Mick. "I'm finding out what it's like to be a priest. I can't remember any time since the Rolling Stones started that I've gone so long without seeing a woman."

above August 18, 1969: Keith and Anita leave King's College Hospital, London, with baby son Marlon, born ten days earlier.

right August 30, 1969: While Mick was filming *Ned Kelly*, Marsha Hunt was insisting she was going to appear topless at the Isle of Wight Pop Festival. Instead, she wowed the crowd with tight-fitting leather hot pants.

right July 10, 1969: Allen Klein pictured in the immediate aftermath of Brian Jones' death. He, too, would soon be ousted from the Stones' set-up, a situation prompted in part by his decision to take over the Beatles' management earlier in the year.

far right October 17, 1969: Despite spending just one day in London between vacationing in Indonesia and flying to America, Mick organized this photo-opportunity to emphasize the Rolling Stones' new businesslike ways.

below The Stones left Heathrow Airport on October 17, 1969 for their first American tour since 1966. On arrival, the band were greeted by a storm over the high ticket prices—but the shows were phenomenal.

babies, babes, business

"The Rolling Stones have never been the most conventional people in the world."

Daily Mirror

AFTER KEITH RICHARD flew back from the United States on December 8, his girlfriend Anita Pallenberg greeted him with the news that her stay in Britain had been extended, at least until October 6, 1970. Anita, who had an Italian passport, said: "I asked for a new visa in July but the Home Office have held my passport ever since. They won't let me have it back and they have told me that I must either get married or get out. I think it's disgraceful. I am not going to get married just to suit them. I would like to get married—around 1975."

Back at the couple's home in Cheyne Walk, Chelsea, Keith Richard added: "Rather than do that, I would leave Britain and live abroad. I don't know when we'll marry. I don't want to rush into anything."

Between 1967 and the late seventies, Keith Richard and Anita Pallenberg epitomized everything that was gloriously

"marry or get out"

debauched about the Rolling Stones. They were self-styled rock 'n' roll gypsies who did their best to maintain a Bohemian, twenty-four-hour lifestyle. Their lives were shrouded in rumor and innuendo that a series of mishaps, including drug busts, house fires, and car crashes did little to dispel.

The couple had emerged as central characters in the Stones during 1968, when Anita was filming *Performance* with Mick Jagger and Keith was busy taking full responsibility for the band's musical direction. The movie, shot between September and November, could have severely tested their relationship, not least because of the intimacy Jagger and Pallenberg shared during the shoot. But Keith and Anita were to

above December 8, 1969: Just hours after the show at Altamont, in California, where a fan was stabbed to death in front of the stage, a somber-looking Keith Richard and Charlie Watts return to London.

withstand far sterner tests than that during the course of the next decade.

Keith Richard's emergence as a real force behind the Stones was partly a response to the decline of Brian Jones. He was forced to take on additional duties that Jones, as second guitarist, had neglected, while at the same time maintain that crucial element of wickedness that Jones brought to the band. Quickly perfecting the dashing deviant image that has spawned countless third-rate imitators, Keith soon rivaled Mick as one of the defining figures of rock 'n' roll. Meanwhile Jagger, inspired by playing the character Turner in *Performance*, acquired a full set of personalities which he could select to hide behind at random.

Richard's veil of detachment and Jagger's role-playing gave the Stones a new-found aura of supremacy, which, in turn, inspired the band to new creative heights. The results could be clearly heard on *Let It Bleed*, their November 1969 follow-up to the *Beggars Banquet* album. The opening chords of the first track, "Gimme Shelter," which crept up on the listener like a sickness, were full of foreboding. The chorus was no more comforting, either as Jagger warned: "Rape, murder, it's just a shot away!"

"Gimme Shelter" set the tone of the entire record, which was leaner and meaner than any previous Stones album, with some suitably decadent lyric contributions from Jagger—about drugs, groupies, sex, and death. Unfortunately, the band's flirtations with the dark side rebounded on them on the night of December 6, 1969 at the end of their American tour. A farewell open-air, free concert at the Altamont Speedway, outside San Francisco, turned into the biggest nightmare of the band's career. One fan was stabbed to death in front of the

"I refuse to get married because some bureaucrat says we must."

Keith Richard

 **above** Anita Pallenberg and four-month-old son, Marlon, were at the airport to meet them.

far right Back in their Chelsea home, Keith and Anita celebrate the Home Office's decision to allow her to stay in Britain until at least October 6, 1970.

stage, and the event was captured on film and included in the fascinating documentary of the tour, also titled *Gimme Shelter*.

The band had flown out to the United States on October 17, uncertain of the reception that would greet them. After all, they'd not toured there since 1966, and plenty had happened during the intervening years, including the hippie revolution and the politicization of American youth. In fact, the tour proved to be a huge success,

with sell-out shows across the country and the Stones turning in some of the best performances of their career. Why not, suggested Jagger, hold a free show at Altamont as "a Christmas present to our American fans."

Unfortunately, the goodwill gesture backfired horribly. On the advice of the San Francisco groups, the local Hell's Angels were hired to provide security at the show, and were provided with free beer as pay-

ment. That, combined with a batch of bad acid and a strangely downbeat atmosphere, set off a virtual war between the Angels and the fans who'd gathered at the front of the stage. The day was punctuated with beatings, as "security" waded in with fists and billiard cues, but when 18-year-old Meredith Hunter was stabbed to death during the Stones' set, many tried to lay the blame on the band for unlocking these strange, violent forces.

homecoming

"British fans politely applaud Mick Jagger." *Daily Mirror*

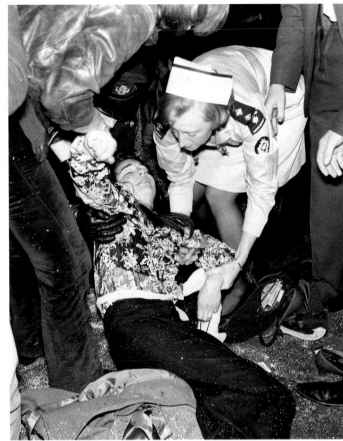

facing page Among the seated audience were (from left) Charlie Watts' wife Shirley, actor Sir John Geilgud, and movie director Tony Richardson, who'd recently worked with Mick Jagger on *Ned Kelly*.

above Despite police fears, the audience was impeccably behaved. Mick Jagger was disappointed: "Get up and dance, won't you?" he urged. A handful took to the aisles. "The rest watched sheepishly," reported the *Daily Mirror*.

above right December 21, 1969: There was a little more drama at the Lyceum, in London, a few days later, where crash barriers were erected and fans fainted at the show's climax.

inset December 18, 1969: The estranged Mick and Marianne, protected by Les Perrin, their cigar-chomping PR man, return to court to face charges of cannabis possession.

A S NEWS OF THE TRAGIC Altamont concert filtered home, the authorities decided to place an additional police presence at the band's homecoming shows, held at two central London venues, the Saville Theatre and the Lyceum. Ten police officers were posted to the Saville, while the orchestra and circle were discreetly ringed by thirty-two strong-arm men. An emergency ward was set up in the ladies' lavatories where fifteen St. John Ambulance Brigade members remained on standby. Chief Inspector Dennis Chapman told reporters: "We are here, basically, to see that no one is born improperly, or dies illegally." Happily, the *Daily Mirror* reported that "the guards needn't have bothered … The audience of 1,200 greeted the Stones with British enthusiasm. They clapped."

The Stones' live set had altered dramatically since the band's last indoor London show in September 1966. Many old favorites had been dropped, and the ones that stayed—like Chuck Berry's "Carol," "Under My Thumb," and "(I Can't Get No) Satisfaction"—had been rejuvenated by the urgent twin-guitar assault of Keith Richard and Mick Taylor. This new team had really begun to gel, particularly on the newer

material. Their guitars interlocked with genuine malevolence during "Midnight Rambler," Jagger's Boston Strangler-inspired *pièce de résistance*, during which he'd sadistically whip the stage with his leather belt. They traded fierce, lengthy solos during "Sympathy For The Devil," and shows reached an almighty, cacophonous climax as the guitarists sparred during "Street Fighting Man." It was an ideal show-closer and the perfect way to see out what had been a tumultuous decade.

The Rolling Stones had changed, and so had their audience. Back in 1966, when

they'd last toured the country, the Stones were package-tour headliners delivering half-hour sets to audiences of screaming girls who could barely hear what the band were playing. By the end of 1969, pop had grown up. It was now called rock, and to show their maturity, crowds sat and listened as new equipment filled large concert halls with ear-splitting sound. They'd come to see great artistry and technical ability unfold before them—although the rock 'n' rolling Stones were never entirely convinced by rock's new seriousness. Mick Jagger, the consummate rock frontman, understood that every audience, however, po-faced, still desired spectacle.

A performance he would have preferred not to have given took place on December 18 at the Marlborough Street Magistrates Court, in London, when he arrived with Marianne Faithfull to face drug possession charges arising from the bust earlier in the year. By now, the increasingly fragile Marianne had left Jagger and moved to Rome to live with Italian movie director Mario Schifano. Mick was bruised, and shortly after the court appearance, wooed her back after a face-to-face confrontation with the pair in Italy.

Chapter Six 1970–72
JETSET PLAYBOYS

THE STONES, RUDDERLESS POP MISCREANTS just three years earlier, had by 1970 completed a dramatic transformation that held them in good stead for the new decade. That year, which saw the Beatles split and new rock icons Jimi Hendrix and Janis Joplin dying prematurely, found the Stones reemerging with sufficient longevity and credibility to pass themselves off as "the Greatest Rock 'n' Roll Band in the World" without anyone—a few Led Zeppelin fans notwithstanding—doubting their claim.

That particular epithet introduced the band's classic live album, *Get Yer Ya-Ya's Out!*, which documented their thrilling comeback tour of the United States the previous winter. They promoted it with a two-month tour of Europe during the fall, and that was virtually it for the Stones during 1970, although behind the scenes, they were busy laying plans that would be fully realized in the months ahead.

> "For the first time in their career, the Stones, and Mick Jagger in particular, were in the driving-seat."

Having reestablished their career on a sound musical footing, the band made moves to guarantee the business side of their activities was in good health. The Stones, like so many sixties artists, realized they hadn't always received the money they were entitled to, due to a mixture of naivety and a youthful disregard for financial matters. By 1970, they'd finally tired of watching others grow fat on the fruits of their endeavors.

And so it was that the Rolling Stones became international playboys. By 1971, they'd extricated themselves from Decca, the record company with whom they'd always endured a particularly fragile relationship, and from Allen Klein's ABKCO management company. For the first time in their career, the Stones, and Mick Jagger in particular, were in the driving seat. They formed their own record company, Rolling Stones Records, and on the advice of their new business manager, moved away from Britain in the spring to avoid the high tax rates that hampered their new-found businesslike style. ■

left Mick and Nicaraguan model Bianca sport central American headgear on a rainy day in Newcastle, England. Much was made of the couple's striking facial similarities.

111

1970–72

The Stones have big ideas for their own record label. "We want to release the odd blues record and Charlie Watts wants to do some jazz. What we're not interested in is bubblegum material," insists Mick Jagger.

When John Dunbar files for divorce from his estranged wife Marianne Faithfull in September 1970, he cites Mick Jagger as corespondent. No one is surprised, least of all Mick, who is ordered to pay costs of £200.

Eric Clapton and Al Kooper join Keith Richard for his 27th birthday party, which takes place at Olympic Studios, in London, on December 18, 1970. The proceedings inevitably turn into a jam session and the makeshift lineup run through a spirited version of a new song, "Brown Sugar."

After Decca release an album of old Stones recordings, the band take out full-page ads in the music press urging fans to boycott the record claiming that: "It is, in our opinion, below the standard we try to keep up, both in choice of content and cover design."

While in France, Mick Jagger rents a house in Mougins, home of Pablo Picasso. Meanwhile, Bill Wyman strikes up a friendship with another legendary artist, Marc Chagall.

On May 5, 1971, Bianca tells the *Daily Mirror*: "There's not going to be a wedding this week, next week, or ever. Mick and I are very happy together. We don't need to get married. Why should we?" A week later they were married.

Gone but not forgotten. Tapes recorded by Brian Jones in Morocco were released on the new Rolling Stones record label in October 1971 as *Brian Jones Presents The Pipes Of Pan At Joujouka*.

Carly Simon's 1972 hit single, "You're So Vain," features Mick Jagger on backing vocals. Although this suggests the song is about him, the prime suspect is actor Warren Beatty. Carly shows up at Mick's 29th birthday party after the Stones' performance at New York's Madison Square Garden.

cleanup time

TWO LONG-TERM, on–off relationships sorted themselves out during the early months of 1970. Mick Jagger's three-and-a-half-year affair with Marianne Faithfull came to an untidy, if barely noticed, conclusion; more importantly, the Rolling Stones ended their increasingly bitter business association with Allen Klein. As it turned out, they couldn't completely disengage themselves from the tough New Yorker, but at least they were now able to control their current affairs without ABKCO's involvement.

The writing had been on the wall for Mick and Marianne since late 1968. While Jagger had begun to mix post-hippie hedonism with a keen desire to direct the Rolling Stones' business empire, Marianne became farther removed from anything resembling stability. Ironically, the outcome of the couple's January 26, 1970 court case, which stemmed from a drug bust at Cheyne Walk the previous May, was that Jagger received a fine, while Marianne, whose life now revolved around hard drugs, walked from the court unblemished.

She returned briefly to her new lover, Italian movie producer Mario Schifano, a liaison that was widely regarded as a way of

below January 26, 1970: The new decade began much as the old one ended —with Mick and Marianne surrounded by crowds and press photographers as they made their way to court to face yet another drug charge.

The second great parting was even messier. In spring 1970, the Beatles had split amid much acrimony. While Allen Klein, whom Mick Jagger had recommended to John Lennon, was embroiled in the battle to clear up the mess, Jagger made his move. Recruiting the pin-striped City banker Prince Rupert Loewenstein to handle the band's finances, the Stones announced their split with Klein on July 29: "Neither Allen Klein nor ABKCO Industries Inc., nor any other company have any authority to negotiate recording contracts on [our] behalf in the future." Klein's office retorted with a claim that the announcement wouldn't alter his company's "rights" under any existing agreements.

It took two years to secure an amicable peace: In a joint announcement on May 10, 1972, it was declared that ABKCO were no longer the business managers of the Rolling Stones. However, the band soon discovered that Klein could still exercise a hold on the group's career when a live album from the 1972 U.S. tour was halted after ABKCO refused the Stones permission to include a handful of pre-1970 songs—to which Klein still owned the publishing rights.

While battling Klein, the Rolling Stones doggedly sought to protect their current and future earnings by negotiating a new record deal, and made plans to head off a huge tax bill, which had built up over years of neglect. (In May 1970, for example, it was announced that Brian Jones was more than £100,000 in debt when he died.) Prince Rupert advised the group that by living abroad for most of the following financial year, they could avoid paying British taxes; from September 1970, plans were made for the great Rolling Stones exodus.

Meanwhile, the band's first manager Andrew Oldham had proved less durable than either Klein or the Stones, and despite a roster that included Humble Pie and the Small Faces, his Immediate record company had fallen on hard times. One of pop's most flamboyant managers quietly slipped into obscurity.

above April 9, 1970: Allen Klein at the Beatles' Apple offices in Saville Row, London. While preoccupied with the Beatles' split, Klein was ousted as the Stones' business manager, although he retained control over the group's sixties recordings.

"It really is disgusting albums making so much money."

Mick Jagger, *Melody Maker*

punishing Jagger for his negligence and preoccupation with Stones business. When Mick and Marianne united once more in March 1970, the spurned Schifano quipped: "I suppose they're inseparable. After all they were together a long time." But Jagger seemed remarkably underwhelmed by the reunion, telling reporters: "We are still good friends and I hope that we shall remain so."

Inevitably, the reconciliation didn't last long. In mid-June, Marianne left Mick's home in Cheyne Walk for the last time, and within weeks she was being linked with Lord Patrick Rossmore, a 39-year-old Irish photographer. Months later, she was propping up a wall in Great Windmill Street, just off London's Piccadilly Circus, waiting for her next fix. Shortly after the split, Mick Jagger's name was being linked with Patti D'Arbanville, a 19-year-old New York model.

left May 3, 1970: Andrew Oldham (right) and business partner Tony Calder ponder their futures after the collapse of their record company, Immediate.

strip Mick and Marianne's recent reconciliation wasn't strong enough to preserve the most glamorous relationship of the late sixties, and by the summer of 1970, Faithfull had walked out on the Stone for good.

a family affair

"I'll never settle down. I'm not the type."

Mick Jagger

facing page August 28, 1970: Anita Pallenberg, Mick Jagger, and Keith Richard (with son Marlon), probably the three most powerful figures in the Rolling Stones camp during the seventies.

above Bill Wyman, his wife Astrid and eight-year-old son Steven, fly out on New Year's Eve 1970 for a skiing vacation in Sweden. Overworked throughout the previous decade, the Stones gave themselves more free time during the seventies.

left Mick Taylor and his girlfriend, 22-year-old Rose Miller—proud parents of "Chloe, the new Rolling Stones baby".

below Once it was Mick and Marianne. Now Keith and Anita set the tone for the public's perception of the Stones. The pair juggled domesticity with a lifestyle dedicated to stretching the bounds of conventional morality.

Stones to quit UK?

JUST HOURS BEFORE the Rolling Stones opened their first national tour of Britain since 1966, rumors that they were about to leave Britain to live in France were confirmed. Their publicity agent Les Perrin told reporters: "The move to the south of France has been in the air for some time. Now it is definite. I shouldn't be surprised if they leave within the next couple of months.

"It has taken the boys months to arrange to emigrate," Perrin continued. "They have had long and complicated talks with lawyers and financial advisers, but the real reason they are leaving this country is that they like France—and the climate is so much better." He added that the group will continue to record in England and will retain their British citizenship. Just hours before the first show at Newcastle City Hall, Mick

Jagger insisted: "It's only for the change of scenery and temperature. I love Britain. I just want a change. We will probably be back more often than we have in the past."

Once again, the newspapers expressed surprise that audiences at Rolling Stones concerts no longer screamed. In fact, reported the *Daily Mirror* on March 5, 1971, "During most of the numbers, the audience—with boys outnumbering girls—sat

left The two Roundhouse shows were the band's last public performances in Britain until September 1973. A cast of superstars, including Eric Clapton, and Rod Stewart and the Faces, turned out to see them.

above Fans line up outside London's notorious hippie venue, the Roundhouse in Chalk Farm, for a last glimpse of the band before the Stones emigrate to the south of France.

far left The Stones had become a lean, mean machine by the time of the whistle-stop March 1971 British tour. They premiered songs from the forthcoming *Sticky Fingers* album, including the later No. 1 hit, "Brown Sugar."

"The real reason they are leaving this country is that they like France."

Les Perrin, the Stones' PR man

rapt and intent, just listening … It showed pop fans had grown up." Even Mick Jagger's demand ("I want to see you dance and lose your inhibitions") went unheeded. At the end of the show, "Many gave the two-fingered peace sign with both hands," but there were still no screams.

The tour preceded the release of *Sticky Fingers*, the band's first studio album since 1969's *Let It Bleed*. The delay wasn't simply

down to the fall-out with Klein or the tax-inspired move to France. The Rolling Stones' contract with Decca Records had expired on July 31, 1970 and the group had no intention of re-signing to a company they regarded as out-of-touch and even mildly contemptuous of its greatest assets. To show his disdain, Mick Jagger recorded one additional contract-filling single for Decca, knowing full well that the company

would never be able to release it. The title? "Cocksucker Blues."

After approaches from EMI, CBS, RCA, and even Decca, it was announced on April 7, 1971 that the Rolling Stones had signed to Atlantic Records—with the added kudos that they were now able to release disks on their own Rolling Stones Records imprint. The band's new commerce-meets-creativity world was falling into place.

and Bianca comes too

right March 4, 1971: An early glimpse of Mick Jagger's new girlfriend "Blanca Marcas" (*sic*) as the pair arrive at Newcastle Central Station for the first concert of the Stones' spring 1971 British tour.

A T THE END OF the Stones' fall 1970 European tour, Mick Jagger flew into Heathrow with a "mystery woman" by his side. "What's your name?" asked a reporter. "I have no name. I do not speak English," came the reply. "We're just good friends," explained Mick helpfully. It was a teasing start for a relationship that would fill the gossip columns for the next decade —and threaten the very existence of the Rolling Stones in the process.

The mystery woman was one Bianca Pérez Morena de Macías, of indeterminate age, wealth, and origin. She was first introduced to Jagger midway through the Stones' fall 1970 European tour, after the band's Paris Olympia show on September 22. From that moment, until she became Mrs Bianca Jagger in a hastily arranged ceremony in St.-Tropez, France, on May 13, 1971, the dark-haired, Nicaraguan beauty remained by Mick's side. Even Jagger's aides were surprised at the singer's new-found devotion to one woman. He punched

"I'm not the sort of bloke who would make a big fuss of announcing a date, am I?"

Mick Jagger, *Daily Mirror*

photographers who intruded on their privacy and, particularly after Bianca became pregnant in the spring of 1971, he constantly missed band meetings, including recording sessions for the *Exile On Main Street* album, to be by her side. The couple's daughter, Jade, was born on October 21, 1971.

This might have made life within the Stones more difficult; but from the fans' point of view, Jagger's new-found happiness had no adverse effect on the group's music. During the March 1971 tour, the group—now joined on stage by horn players Jim Price and Bobby Keyes, plus keyboard man Nicky Hopkins—previewed some of the new material, including two rousing, if misogynistic anthems, "Brown Sugar" and "Bitch." Shortly afterward, "Brown Sugar," the first release on Rolling Stones Records, gave the Stones their first No. 1 hit single of the seventies.

The accompanying *Sticky Fingers* album, rudely dressed in a Andy Warhol-designed sleeve featuring an obviously male, denim-clad crotch, complete with real-life zipper-fly, also lived up to expectations, blending full-blooded rock 'n' roll with some of the most sophisticated work of the band's career. Two of the finest songs, "Wild Horses" and "Sister Morphine," were touching tributes to Marianne Faithfull; the closing "Moonlight Mile" was a heady, orchestral-driven piece; while "Can't You Hear Me Knocking" gave Mick Taylor the chance to display his virtuoso guitar skills. It was the perfect riposte to the cries of "Sell out!" that occasionally greeted the Stones during the spring 1971 concerts.

top, middle and right March 12, 1971: Keith Richard with medicine chest in one hand, cigarette in the other—and yet these eager fans still demand autographs before the Liverpool Empire performance later that evening.

above March 4, 1971: Mick Jagger talks to the press before the Stones' Newcastle City Hall show. The hot story was the band's intention to move abroad, widely seen as a way of avoiding Britain's redistributive tax system.

"I had a couple of grand in the bank, a car, and two houses, but I owed the Inland Revenue a fortune."

Bill Wyman

rolling in it!

facing page, top Bill Wyman purchased Gedding Hall, a fourteen-acre estate near Bury St. Edmunds in Suffolk, England, in September 1968. In light of the Stones' decision to live abroad, Bill and his family were forced to leave it behind for a house in the south of France.

facing page, below left Peckhams, Charlie Watt's thirteenth-century farmhouse in Halland, outside Lewes, Sussex. When Charlie bought his first vintage home in 1965, his father said: "We can't understand why he prefers an old place to something modern."

facing page, below right While the rest of the band owned country estates, Mick Taylor was still flat-bound, albeit in Montrose Place, based in London's fashionable Belgravia district.

top left Charlie Watts' wife Shirley tends to one of the couple's beloved horses. Watts' other private passions include jazz, art, and collecting books and memorabilia on the American Civil War.

left The driveway toward Keith Richard's Redlands home in Sussex. Protected by a high brick wall, barbed wire, huge wooden gates, and a moat, the house also had an intercom system built into the outer wall.

Exile on the Riviera

N APRIL 1971, the Rolling Stones left behind their palatial estates in the English countryside to take up residence in the south of France. The Mediterranean coastline became their base for the next eighteen months, during which time they recorded their only studio double-album set, *Exile On Main Street*—and, of course, saved a few pounds in taxes at the same time.

Nellcote, Keith and Anita's huge, Roman-style villa on a hill above Villefranche-sur-Mer, soon became the band's HQ, playing host to a variety of hangers-on and the Rolling Stones Mighty Mobile, a £100,000, state-of-the-art sixteen-track recording studio, which enabled the band to record their next album, in the basement of the house. When not recording or entertaining huge numbers of friends for what the French police later suspected were "drugs and sex orgies," Keith and Anita cruised the Mediterranean on their yacht, which they'd playfully christened the *Mandrax*.

Not everyone welcomed the mass migration. Bill Wyman and Charlie Watts were always the home-loving Stones, although Bill sought to make the most of their self-imposed exile by building a £400,000 chalet in the hills just outside Cannes. (The rest of the band rented properties.)

Worse was to come for the two "quiet" Stones: After tales of debauchery at Richard's Nellcote house reached the French authorities, the pair, the only two band members in the country at the time, were arrested in September 1972. Wyman and Watts were subsequently cleared of any involvement, although Keith and Anita were fined 5,000 francs apiece the following October for hosting drugs parties. The case brought the Rolling Stones' French sojourn to an abrupt and unhappy close.

"If I go back and live there, it'll be in Buckingham Palace."

Keith Richard

Keith Richard and Anita Pallenberg's south of France residence bore all the trappings of Hollywood-by-the-sea, and domestic scenes such as these

leaving on a jet plane

"We tour so we can make music together. The other groups stopped playing together, and you saw what happened ... "

Charlie Watts

Terry Southern, artist Andy Warhol and Princess Lee Radziwill, joined the entourage together with an army of drug dealers and groupies. It was probably the most decadent traveling circus ever, captured in all its warts 'n' all glory in Robert Frank's infamous *Cocksucker Blues* movie. The band later had second thoughts about the film—which features drug-taking, sex orgies, and a flying television set—and it's only ever been screened at special events.

Despite the mayhem that surrounded it, the tour was highly organized, with the group traveling from city to city in a private jet, taking their own especially designed stage with them. In that respect, America '72 was the first of the monumental Rolling Stones tours.

Musically, there was a greater sense of fun than there had been on the '69 tour, although some critics suggested the band's performances—and Jagger's in particular—came dangerously close to parody at times. True, Jagger had upped the camp element of his act, strutting around in his stars-and-stripes top hat and indulging in mock on-stage sparring with the rest of the band, but with new songs like "Rocks Off," "Rip This Joint," "Tumbling Dice," and

"Happy" (which gave Keith Richard a rare opportunity to take center stage) slotting neatly alongside more established classics, the sell-out shows were as musically thrilling as ever.

Evidence of a growing creative gulf between Mick Jagger and Keith Richard began to show during sessions for the next album, *Goats Head Soup*. Infected by the emerging reggae sounds they heard (which Keith Richard claimed was "the new blues"), the group had decamped en masse in winter 1972 to Kingston, Jamaica, in search of new inspiration. It was the beginning of a musical love affair for Keith, but the venture yielded mixed results for the Stones.

If there was a moment when the band had slipped quietly into parody, it was on "Dancing With Mr. D," a mock-demonic remake of "Jumpin' Jack Flash" and the album's opening track. Elsewhere on the record, the band journeyed into funk ("100 Years Ago"), mock-psychedelia ("Can You Hear The Music"), and new-spun ballads ("Coming Down Again," "Winter," "Angie"), although in spite of these new adventures, it was hard to ignore the record's downbeat mood.

facing page May 25, 1972: Keith Richard and Mick Jagger in relaxed mood as a major, two-month-long American tour looms ahead.

strip March 2, 1972: Charlie Watts, his wife Shirley, and their three-year-old daughter Serafina, leave Heathrow for Nice, in France, via Paris.

above left May 25, 1972: A cane-wielding Jagger orchestrates another eventful Stones departure at Heathrow, watched by his wife Bianca.

above middle May 25, 1972: Mick Taylor and his girlfriend Rose, minutes before the guitarist boards a plane bound for the United States.

above right Bill Wyman, returning home from the West Indies in November 1972 with his wife Astrid.

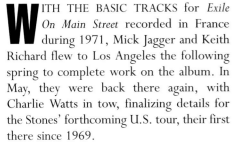

WITH THE BASIC TRACKS for *Exile On Main Street* recorded in France during 1971, Mick Jagger and Keith Richard flew to Los Angeles the following spring to complete work on the album. In May, they were back there again, with Charlie Watts in tow, finalizing details for the Stones' forthcoming U.S. tour, their first there since 1969.

The two-month jaunt, during June and July 1972, was an altogether happier affair than their previous visit. Celebrities, including writers Truman Capote and

Chapter Seven 1973–74
TRIUMPHANT RETURN

WHEN THE ROLLING STONES FLEW IN for their 1973 British tour, their first domestic dates since March 1971, the mood was one of triumphant celebration. It had been ten years since the band's first hit, "Come On," and the press went into "Will this be the last time?" overdrive. The tour could have sold out several times over, ample proof that despite the advances of hard rock heroes like Led Zeppelin and Deep Purple, and new glam rock stars like Marc Bolan and David Bowie, the Rolling Stones remained without peers.

The band that began as R&B purists, that dismissed white pop as chewing-gum for the ears, had proved to be musical chameleons of the first order. In the face of psychedelia, hard rock, and now glam rock, the Stones had survived wave after wave of

"Jagger paraded around the stage with all the enthusiasm of a teenager on heat."

new-fangled fads and fashions. Ironically, just as they were being celebrated for their remarkable staying power, they'd begun to falter musically—although in all the surrounding publicity, few noticed.

What they saw instead was Mick Jagger, dressed in a sparkling costume that both acknowledged and parodied glam rock, parading around the stage with all the enthusiasm of a teenager on heat. Mick Taylor excepted, the Rolling Stones had reached the grand old age of 30, but Jagger wasn't prepared to give in to his youthful rivals just yet. Reporters dug up an old quote where he claimed he'd retire when he reached 30, and while the singer was astute enough to realize that fueling the guessing game was good for business, he was clearly enjoying himself too much to seriously entertain the idea. "Maybe when I'm 33," he teased.

After touring for much of 1973, the Stones retreated to the recording studio. They emerged the following summer with a new album, *It's Only Rock 'n' Roll*, a more upbeat and friendlier affair than *Goats Head Soup*, but one that again lacked the flair and majesty of, say, *Sticky Fingers* or *Exile On Main Street*. But other matters were on their minds, not least the faltering loyalty of guitarist Mick Taylor and the media-hogging antics of Mick's wife Bianca. ■

left When the Stones rolled back into Britain for a summer 1973 tour, they held a party at Blenheim Palace, home of the Duke of Marlborough, pictured here with rock aristo Mick Jagger.

1973–74

During the Stones' tour of Australia early in 1973, the Immigration Minister Albert Grassby says: "The Rolling Stones are an excellent example to Australian youth. I have no regrets that I let them in. Yes, I went out on a limb to give them visas. To give a man a bad name and hang him is immoral and un-Australian."

The major controversy surrounding the forthcoming *Goats Head Soup* album is the inclusion of a song originally titled "Starfucker", but amended at the record company's behest to "Star Star". The original title is still heard throughout the song, which also includes a line about "giving head to Steve McQueen". The actor approved.

1973's rumours include Keith Richard getting a complete blood change at a Swiss clinic; Mick and Bianca's marriage already on the rocks; and the Rolling Stones and the Faces joining forces as the ultimate supergroup.

The Stones are prevented from entering Japan because of Mick Jagger's 1967 drug conviction, which leaves a huge gap in the band's Far East touring schedule. "The main thing that bugs us is that we got nothing to do for ten days. It's not a great financial loss," claims Jagger.

Left-wing agitators protest outside the group's concert in Berlin, claiming that ticket prices are too high and that the group are "capitalist pigs". Over 1000 riot police are sent in to quell the demonstration.

Mick Jagger's younger brother Chris makes his recording debut with an album for G&R Records. Mick helps out on a couple of tracks but it's not enough to make the record a hit.

David Bailey's cover photo for *Goats Head Soup* prompts much speculation. Mick Jagger, his head covered by a veil, is said to bear an uncanny resemblance to his ex, Marianne Faithfull.

Mick Taylor's departure in December 1974 prompts a flurry of rumours about a replacement. Names put forward include Ron Wood, Jeff Beck, Mick Ronson and Harvey Mandel.

quake rock

O N 23 DECEMBER 1972, a massive earthquake destroyed much of Nicaragua's capital city Managua, leaving a reported 6000 people dead. Hearing the news while preparing to spend a quiet Christmas together at home in Cheyne Walk, Mick and Bianca Jagger immediately changed their plans – Bianca's mother was missing and uncontactable.

The pair travelled to the ravaged city on 28 December in a specially chartered private jet, taking 2000 anti-typhoid injections with them. Arriving in the disaster-struck zone, the Jaggers then made several appeals on local radio and eventually located Bianca's mother, Mrs Macías, along with several relatives, sheltering in the nearby town of Leon.

The first-hand experience of the devastation clearly affected Mick, who broke with tradition by hastily arranging a benefit concert featuring the Stones. The show took place at the Los Angeles Forum on 18 January 1973, with support from the west coast's own Latin expatriates Santana and comedy duo Cheech and Chong.

Over 18,000 fans packed the auditorium, braving the worst weather witnessed in the city for months, in order to take up their seats – priced at between $10 and

$100. After a minute's silence in memory of the earthquake victims, a Nicaraguan flag was unfurled (to hang alongside the Stones' notable "tongue" logo) and the event got underway. The Stones walked out to a barrage of white lights, with Jagger fetchingly dressed in a multi-layered costume. Gradually casting aside his mask, cape, tiara and denim jacket, he soon stripped down to a sky-blue "celestial" velvet jumpsuit studded with silver sequins. The longer the concert went on, the more flesh his unzipped costume revealed.

The band broke a second rule for the show, too – by playing an encore. After a set that had consisted of the usual mix of vintage material like "Route 66" and "It's All Over Now", with more recent

this and facing page The Stones made a rare exception to their own "no charity events" rule after an earthquake in December 1972 destroyed Managua, Bianca's birthplace in Nicaragua. The benefit show took place at the Forum in Los Angeles on 18 January.

songs, the band returned for a lengthy version of "Midnight Rambler", complete with Jagger's usual stage-whipping sequence. After another banner was unwrapped to reveal a parting "Thank You" message, the audience filed out to the sounds of "Greensleeves" playing over the PA.

The goodwill didn't stop there. Mick Jagger later put the studded velvet costume he'd worn for the show up for auction, adding the personal inscription: "To the owner, much love, Mick Jagger". After expenses had been deducted, the concert raised $352,274, and on 9 May 1973, Mick flew into Washington to hand the cheque over to the Nicaraguan authorities. As late as November 1974, the Jaggers returned to Managua to monitor the proper distribution of the funds raised.

Meanwhile, the music scene was rapidly changing, especially at home, where glam rock – essentially a back-to-basics, three-chord style dressed up in sparkly threads – had revitalized the moribund pop charts. Since the demise of the Beatles, all the action had been happening in the LP market, which was dominated by bands that appealed largely to students and young adults. Ranging from the thunderous heavy metal of Led Zeppelin, Black Sabbath and Deep Purple to the sophisticated soundscapes of Pink Floyd, the emphasis was strictly anti-pop, with songs sometimes stretched into 20-minute epics and the groups invariably dressed in drab denim.

Glam rock changed all that. Musically unsophisticated, it was thoroughly dismissed by the self-appointed taste-makers. But it brought an element of fun back into pop, not least in elevating the likes of Marc Bolan and David Bowie (both of whom had spent years in obscurity) into superstars. The Stones cleverly managed to steer a course midway between these two opposing styles, with a combination of rock sophistication and showbiz glamour that managed to satisfy audiences old and new. A delicately maintained balance, it helped sustain the group's popularity through to the next musical explosion – punk rock in 1976.

"The longer the concert went on, the more flesh his unzipped costume revealed."

Redlands ablaze

A MYSTERIOUS FIRE ON JULY 31, 1973 destroyed much of Redlands, Keith Richard's beloved hideaway home in West Wittering, Sussex. The blaze came just weeks after a mysterious fire at Stargroves, Mick Jagger's country home.

Richard and girlfriend Anita Pallenberg carried their children, Marlon, three, and 15-month-old Dandelion, to safety as the thatched roof of the twelfth-century farmhouse went up in flames. Then the

worth £50,000 now." But he vowed to restore the building, parts of which date back to 1137, and in October 1974, an application to restore the property was duly lodged with the local authorities. Later, it was suggested the fire was probably caused when Keith fell asleep while smoking a cigarette.

It wasn't Keith and Anita's year. Weeks earlier, on June 26, they were busted together with Prince Stanislaus Klossowski

drug and firearm offenses, the Stone was let out on £1,000 bail the following day, and was due to appear at Marlborough Street Magistrates Court in London on October 24.

The case hung over the couple during the Stones' European tour that summer, and it was a relieved Keith Richard who walked free after the hearing, having been handed a £205 fine. "I am delighted," he said. "It's cool." Mr. Richard Du Cann, his

"It's a terrible thing to have happened to such a beautiful place. It's probably worth £50,000 now."

Keith Richard

guitarist, barefoot and wearing shorts and a smoke-stained sweatshirt, helped to carry furniture into the garden while the Chichester Fire Brigade tackled the blaze. The couple were on a whistle-stop visit to collect some belongings from the country retreat when the fire broke out.

While Anita stood in the front yard, her clothes dripping with water, Keith Richard told reporters: "It may have been due to an electrical fault—we don't know for certain. It's a terrible thing to have happened to such a beautiful place. It's probably

when police, led by Detective Inspector Charles O'Hanlon, raided their London home. Keith and Anita were in the master bedroom asleep in their four-poster bed; underneath, police found various quantities of drugs, including Mandrax and heroin. They also netted a .38 Smith & Wesson revolver (a gift from an American security guard), an antique shotgun, 110 rounds of ammunition, and drug accessories including water pipes, pharmaceutical scales, and a hypodermic needle on top of the lavatory cistern. After being charged with various

lawyer, had successfully claimed that the drugs had been left by others who used the house while the couple lived in the south of France. Discovering the contraband on his return home, Richard had put it in a trunk under his bed to keep it away from his two children. The Mandrax tablets, he claimed, were obtained by Miss Pallenberg while on holiday in Jamaica where it was unnecessary to have a prescription. The Magistrate, Mr. John Hooper, conceded that the defense had thrown a different light on the case and that he was satisfied with the explanation.

"It's nice to see you again —I hope it's mutual."

Mick Jagger

left The fashionably Afro'd American keyboard player Billy Preston joined the Stones for the 1973 European tour. He collaborated with the band during the seventies, briefly supplanting Nicky Hopkins as "the sixth Stone."

facing page Unzipped for action. Mick Jagger flitted between a leather-look biker image and the more effete costumes of glam rock during the Stones summer tour.

stoned!

above Bianca Jagger's haughty air didn't always sit easily with the Stones' long-established unorthodox ways. By the mid-seventies, she was even eclipsing Mick in the gossip columns.

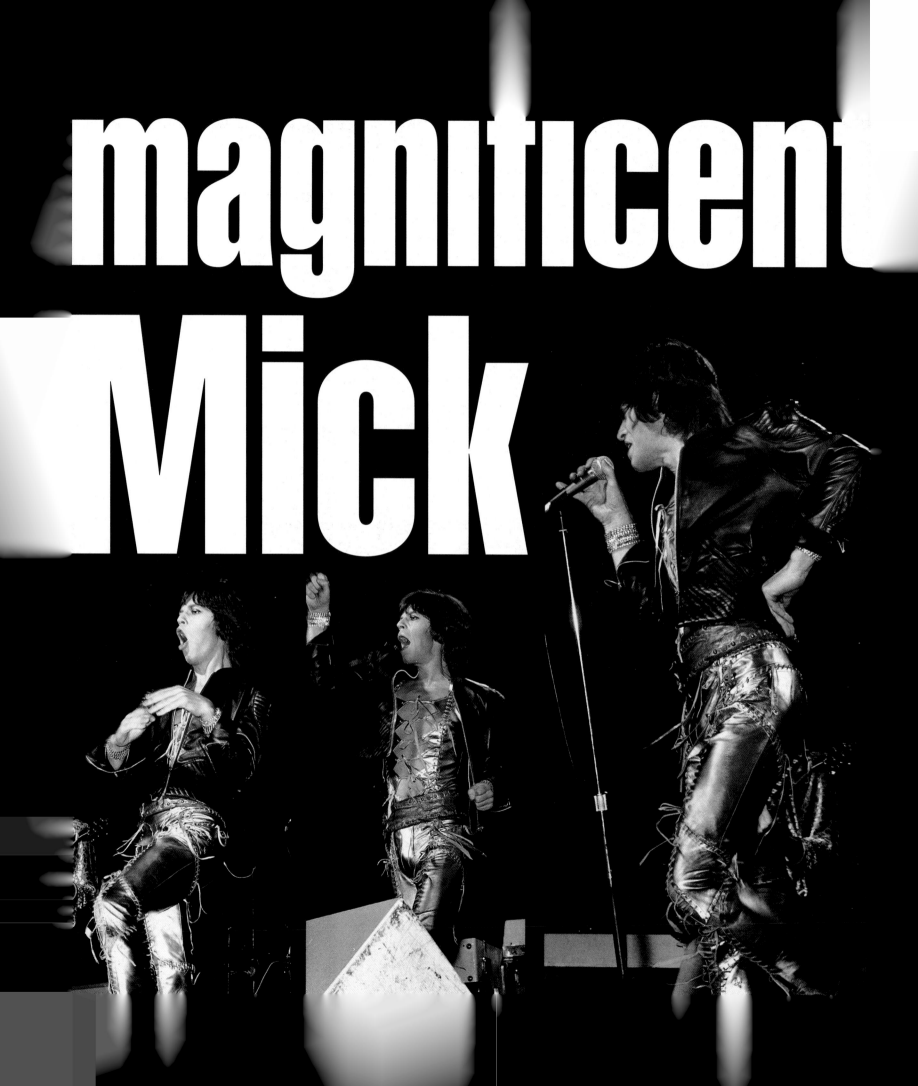

magnificent
Mick

"Mick Jagger is the perfect pop star. There's nobody more perfect than Jagger. He's rude, ugly-attractive, he's brilliant."

Elton John

Having just reached the grand old age of 30, there was considerable speculation that Mick Jagger would soon announce his retirement. But nothing in his stage performances suggested he was about to give up.

IF ANY ONE INDIVIDUAL epitomized the sixties in all its authority-defying, morality-bashing decadence, it was Mick Jagger. The mere sight of him—his surly, mildly unkempt manner exaggerated by lips far too succulent to know the meaning of restraint—was enough to prompt panics in living-rooms up and down Britain. And that was Jagger circa 1964.

As the Stones' popularity increased, his confidence grew—and so did his visibility. By the mid-sixties, Mick's hair-shaking frenzies and James Brown-inspired fancy footwork was augmented by a new-found ability to handle a microphone—and its stand—with menace. With no instrument to concentrate on, he was able to immerse himself completely in the music—and when the sounds the band created started to spin off wildly in all directions, so did Jagger.

More than that, Jagger's lithe, hair-less body introduced a new concept of manhood, far removed from the beef-cake romeos of Hollywood like Robert Mitchum and Rock Hudson. He experimented with makeup, pursed his lips as if preparing to apply a generous stroke of lipstick and hung his wrists on his minuscule hips in a manner that was barely legal.

As time went on, Jagger upped the camp quota in his performances, a move which anticipated the changing times. By now it was the silly, showy, sensational seventies, and the mood of seriousness that had energized teen-agers during the late sixties had collapsed into one uproarious, under-valued, and hopelessly overdressed heap known as glam. For the androgynous Jagger, whose influence on the young David Bowie cannot be exaggerated, it was just another fad that probably wouldn't have happened without him.

from denim to Blenheim

"A knighthood, I'd take nothing less than a knighthood."

Mick Jagger

this and facing page September 6, 1973: As if to confirm that the Stones had become the new royalty, the band threw a party at Blenheim Palace, the home of the Duke of Marlborough. Bianca Jagger (far left) stands in the grounds looking every inch the exotic aristo-wife.

above middle Bianca gets into the party mood with her friend Penelope Tree, model and girlfriend of David Bailey, the British society photographer.

left Unfazed by the event, Keith Richard was probably more concerned about where his next pack of ciggies was coming from, rather than the next plate of canapés.

return to Wembley

IT WAS A SIGN OF THE TIMES that tour manager Peter Rudge gave almost as many interviews as the band, when the Stones rolled into London for the British leg of their summer '73 European tour. Rudge, the 26-year-old Cambridge graduate who'd masterminded the previous year's U.S. tour, was in charge of an operation that comprised an entourage of fifty and some fourteen tons of equipment carried from show to show in two forty-foot trucks. He was the man who knew how many bottles of tequila Keith Richard needed, how much white German wine Charlie Watts required— even the size of Mick Jagger's laundry bill.

The tour opened on September 1 in Vienna, Austria, just as the band's latest single, "Angie," entered the Top 30 and the day after the release of the Stones' new album, *Goats Head Soup*. In many ways, the shows—and the publicity that surrounded them—overshadowed the record, which was subdued by the band's standards. The

facing page September 8, 1973: Crowds gather on a sunny Saturday afternoon for the extra show at the Empire Pool, Wembley, put on due to the unprecedented demand for tickets.

left A lot had changed since fans screamed at the band during the Mad Mod Ball almost a decade ago. By 1973, the crowd were content to sit and muse on the quality of Mick Taylor's increasingly flamboyant guitar solos.

"10,000 pairs of hands applauded Jagger and co.'s mix of theater and musicianship."

band's arrival in Britain on September 5 was followed by a highly publicized homecoming party at Blenheim Palace, the stately home of the Duke of Marlborough, at Woodstock, in Oxfordshire. It was a deliberate ploy to maintain the Stones' distance from their rock 'n' roll rivals, and reinforce their reputation as rock peers.

The bash, which cost in the region of £10,000, was tasteful in the extreme. The rarefied sound of a string quartet perfumed the air, already thick with top-of-the-range aromas exuding from the tangle of *nouveau riche* poseurs and *haute couture* aristo-wives. A variety of circus acts entertained guests around the poolside, which, incidentally, was where the evening's only bit of bad behavior took place, when an inebriated journalist dropped his pants and tried to throw a colleague in. Cakes were iced with the band's tongue logo, but that couldn't hide the fact that most of the Stones looked shy and out-of-place among the 200 guests.

Twenty hours later, the Rolling Stones hit the stage at Wembley, where they'd stolen the show at the Mad Mod Ball almost ten years earlier. Brian Jones was no longer there to compete for the girls' hearts. Neither were many of the girls, for by 1973, the Stones' audience, like that of most rock bands, was predominantly male. Any screams were muted or ironic; instead, the venue vibrated to the sound of 10,000 pairs of hands applauding Jagger and co.'s mix of theater and musicianship. And Jagger and co. was pretty much the sum of

it: The frontman's presence dominated the shows, from Birmingham to Berlin, where the tour ended on October 19.

In the wake of Alice Cooper's nude antics with a snake, and David Bowie's apparent desire to emasculate a generation of teenage boys, the Rolling Stones had, by 1973, become the elder statesmen of debauchery, partially neutered by their age and wealth. But the old whiff of controversy could still rear its head. At the first of four Wembley shows, a group of fans—among the 30,000 or so unlucky enough not to get tickets—battered down a door to gatecrash the concert. Outside, touts were offering tickets with a face value of £2.75 for sale at £15.

At the final Wembley show, a small group of ex-servicemen who were working as security walked out after claiming that Mick Jagger had called them "pigs." "Just think," said one of them, "we fought for the likes of him." Sergeant Major Charles Dawson, who was in charge of the men, told the *Daily Mirror*: "Our job had been to take people to their seats on the arena floor. We had to make sure the gangways were clear as per regulations. One of our men moved a person from the gangway and Mick Jagger shouted: 'xxxx off sergeants. We don't need you.' Then he sang to the audience: 'The sergeants are pigs, the sergeants are pigs.' We have never been treated like this. We are not pigs. He made no attempt at all to apologize. It's the last time we help Mr. Jagger." Jagger later denied that he had sworn at the guards.

above Sergeant Major Charles Dawson, of Kentish Town, London, head of security for the Wembley concerts, was not a happy man. He led a walk-out on the last night after claiming that Mick Jagger had called the guards "pigs."

strip Jagger's showmanship sometimes bordered on parody by 1973, as did some of the band's latest songs, including "Dancing With Mr. D" and "Star Star".

"If you are going to get wasted, then get wasted elegantly."

Keith Richard

left October 24, 1973: Keith and Anita leave Marlborough Street Magistrates Court after being fined £205 on drug and firearm charges. He admitted having heroin, cannabis, a revolver, a shotgun, and ammunition at his Chelsea home. Relatively light sentences were handed out after they claimed the drugs had been left in the house by friends.

facing page, top left Mick Jagger turns up to lend moral support to his increasingly troubled collaborator-in-chief. Richard admitted after the case: "It looked bad for me."

facing page, bottom Keith and Anita arrive at court to face the charges. Behind them (far right) is the ever-flamboyant Prince Stanislaus Klossowski, who was with the pair when the bust occurred.

another day

another bust ....

new faces

above Ronnie Wood outside The Wick, his home in Richmond, Surrey. He told reporters that his romance with ex-Beatle George Harrison's wife Patti Boyd was "definitely on." Wood officially joined the Stones on February 28, 1976.

NERGIZED BY THE 1973 TOUR, the Stones spent a few weeks in Munich, West Germany, during November working on a new album. Revealingly, guitarist Mick Taylor couldn't make it for the sessions. It was the first sign that all was not well within the Stones camp, although it wasn't until December 1974 that Taylor would announce his departure from the group. Meanwhile, Mick Jagger had struck up a friendship with Faces' guitarist Ronnie Wood, whose gritty playing and Keithlike image made him an ideal candidate for any future vacancy in the Stones.

By the summer of 1974, Wood's boundless enthusiasm and easy manner had also won the confidence of Keith Richard, who showed up for Ron's two solo London concerts at the Kilburn Gaumont that July. When Woody's first solo album, *I've Got My Own Album To Do*, appeared weeks later, it included notable contributions from both Jagger and Richard—perhaps by way of thanks for Wood's playing on the Stones' 1974 single, "It's Only Rock 'n' Roll (But I Like It)." It has been suggested that Mick Jagger had initially considered Ron Wood as a replacement for Keith, in the event of the Stones' guitarist being incapacitated due to his close acquaintance with hard drugs, and that may have been one reason why the band stalled over announcing a replacement for Mick Taylor. It was a long time coming,

right November 25, 1973: Mick Jagger and Faces guitarist Ronnie Wood return from Munich where the Stones have been recording material for their new album. Mick Taylor was mysteriously absent from the sessions.

far right, top Marsha Hunt files a paternity suit against Mick Jagger on June 18, 1973, claiming he is the father of her two-year-old daughter Karis. Jagger was formally named as the father in 1979.

far right, bottom July 30, 1974: The night after the death of Mama Cass, Bianca Jagger arrives at the London Palladium to see Debbie Reynolds. Both American entertainers had attended Mick's birthday party four days earlier.

"Mick [Taylor] is a great musician, but he wasn't one of the Rolling Stones."

Ron Wood

but on February 28, 1976, Ronnie Wood officially joined the Rolling Stones.

Another distraction came on June 18, 1973 when Marsha Hunt, unhappy at Mick's neglect of his role as father of her child, filed a paternity suit against him. Hunt had only recently told reporters that "I don't even discuss the father. He was just a friend. We just had a baby. We aren't living together." Jagger, who privately made

no secret of two-year-old Karis's parentage, was incensed by the move, not least because it meant that his own mother discovered the existence of her first grandchild via the newspapers. The judge ordered Mick and Marsha to undergo blood tests, and the matter dragged on until January 1979 when Jagger was formally named as the father and ordered to pay $78,000 a year for Karis's upkeep.

Mick Jagger's "woman troubles" didn't stop there. By 1974, Bianca Jagger was beginning to outflank him in the publicity stakes. Photographers followed her from the fashionable confines of the Tramp night-club in London to the serene sunspots of the Caribbean, charting every outfit, every pout, and, increasingly, every spat with her husband. Highly independent, and not content to become merely "a Stone's wife," Bianca's presence unsettled the group. These were to be rocky years for the band —in 1977 a lengthy jail sentence hung over Keith Richard after a major drug bust in Canada. That same year, punk rock threatened to ruin the career of every rock musician aged 30 and over. But the Stones had seen it all before.

end
of an
era?

July 3, 1974: Five years after his death, many fans, including 24-year-old hairdresser, Margaret Lowe, still flocked to Brian Jones' grave. They came to mourn not only the man, but the flamboyant, idealistic decade he represented.

mick jagger

BEFORE HE BECAME a rhythm and blues enthusiast in his midteens, Michael Philip Jagger, born on July 26, 1943, was a keen sportsman. His father, Joe, was a physical education teacher, and instilled in his eldest son a deep appreciation of cricket, basketball, and athletics. Mick, or Mike as he was known until fame beckoned, attended Maypole Primary Infants School in Dartford, Kent, then Wentworth Junior County Primary School, where he first met Keith Richard.

By 1954, the Jaggers had started to climb up the social scale: They'd moved to a large house in the nearby village of Wilmington; Joe had become director of physical education at a lcoal college; and Mick had passed his eleven-plus exam, and now attended Dartford Grammar School. His diligent attitude to schoolwork, especially history, earned him seven O-level and three A-level exam passes; by fall 1960, he had enrolled in a college course, studying Economics and Political Science at the esteemed London School of Economics. A talented mimic of popular songs, Jagger had also developed a passion for jazz and skiffle music.

That fall, the music-obsessed student was waiting at Dartford Station for his train when he chanced upon an old schoolfriend Keith Richard, who was on his way to Sidcup Art College. Under Jagger's arm was a bundle of rhythm and blues LPs, many purchased by mail order direct from Chess Records in Chicago. Enthused by a shared admiration for R&B, the pair arranged to meet again. Within weeks, they were practicing their own home-grown brand of blues music (with a little rock 'n' roll thrown in for good measure) in a room at the Jagger household. The makeshift combo, who recorded several songs on a reel-to-reel machine, called themselves Little Boy Blue and the Blue Boys. Mick, the most outgoing of the bunch, sang and played harmonica.

keith richard

DELINQUENCY CAME NATURALLY to Keith Richard. In 1956, while at Dartford Technical College, the skinny 13-year-old son of Bert and Doris Richards (he dropped the 's' for professional reasons before reinstating it in the mid-seventies) discovered he much preferred smoking a cigarette in the bike sheds to attending classes. By the time he was packed off to Sidcup Art School, in 1959, he'd discovered a second essential accessory—an electric guitar.

Richard, born on December 18, 1943, acquired his passion for music from his grandfather Gus, a multiinstrumentalist veteran of an interwar-era dance band. During the fifties, Gus amused his young grandson—an only child with six doting aunts—with his old guitar. Keith, who once sang as a choirboy in Westminster Abbey, was eventually given an acoustic guitar of his own for his 15th birthday.

The young truant was eventually dispatched by his parents to Sidcup Art School in Kent (art college was where most ne'er-do-wells ended up), where he enrolled on an advertising course. The liberal atmosphere of art school suited Keith perfectly; he regularly skipped classes so he could practice his guitar-playing.

After that chance meeting with his old schoolmate from Wentworth County Primary in October 1960, Keith joined Mick and a mutual friend, Dick Taylor, for regular sessions, where they'd work up a set of American R&B and rock 'n' roll numbers. Keith's enthusiasm for Chuck Berry was already obvious; songs like "Little Queenie" and "Johnny B. Goode" formed part of the Little Boy Blue and the Blue Boys' repertoire. And the north Kent rhythm and blues fanatics weren't alone in their enthusiasm. On a visit to Alexis Korner's newly formed Ealing Club in London, a haunt for R&B fans, on April 7, 1962, the pair saw a young slide guitarist performing on stage. "Mick and I both thought he was incredible," recalled Keith. His name was Brian Jones.

brian jones

THE ONLY ROLLING STONE not to hail from the London area, Lewis Brian Hopkin-Jones, born on February 28, 1942, came from Cheltenham, a sedate spa town near the Welsh border. The Jones family was staunchly middle class: Brian's father, Lewis, was an aeronautical engineer and organist at his local choral society; his mother Louisa was a piano teacher. Naturally, the Joneses encouraged their son to play the piano. While at Cheltenham Grammar School, 14-year-old Brian decided to switch from piano to wielding a washboard in a local skiffle group; by his mid-teens, he'd become immersed in the more rarefied world of jazz.

Although an impressive, if lazy, student, gaining nine O-level and two A-level exam passes, most of Jones' energies were channeled into music and girls. He learned alto sax, took up the acoustic guitar, and, at 17, made the first of several girlfriends pregnant. That was the cue for Brian to leave home, and he spent some time hitchhiking around Scandinavia. By 1960 he was back in Cheltenham playing in a jazz band, but dreaming of escape. That came after he met London-based blues evangelist Alexis Korner, in town with Chris Barber's Jazz Band. Korner offered him a floor at his London flat, and after the Ealing Club opened its doors in March 1962, Jones—by now styling himself Elmo Lewis—jumped at the chance.

After a liaison with future Manfred Mann vocalist Paul Pond (later Paul Jones), Brian, now permanently based in London, formed a relationship with Mick and Keith that spring. With Brian very much the leader, the trio rehearsed with various musicians above central London pubs like the Bricklayers Arms in Soho and the Wetherby Arms in Chelsea. On July 12, 1962, the fledgling Rollin' Stones made their first performance as the intermission group at the noted Soho jazz venue the Marquee Club.

bill wyman

WILLIAM GEORGE PERKS, the eldest of five, was born into a working-class household in Penge, southeast London, on October 24, 1936. He showed a keen interest in music from a young age, spending several years in a church choir and becoming proficient at clarinet and piano by his early teens. After he won a place at Beckenham Grammar School, Bill also discovered another lifelong pursuit—Crystal Palace Football Club.

When parental pressure forced him to leave school prematurely, Bill became a clerk until military service beckoned in January 1955. He joined the RAF, signing up for an extra year in addition to the compulsory two, and discovered the music of Elvis Presley while stationed in West Germany. One of his friends in the forces was Lee Whyman, the inspiration for Bill's later stage name.

In 1958, Bill was back home in England and dating a local girl, Diane. On October 24, 1959, his 23rd birthday, Bill and Diane, both highly-regarded jive dancers, were married. A thoroughly conventional life beckoned.

All that changed late in 1960 when Bill, an avid follower of pop since the early fifties, bought himself an electric guitar. By mid-1961, he was playing regularly with a local "covers" band, the Cliftons. It was around this time that Bill caught novelty band the Barron Knights in concert; impressed by the group's mighty bass sound, he decided to switch instruments. By fall 1962, it was almost all over for the Cliftons. That December, the band's drummer Tony Chapman invited Bill to a rehearsal for one of his sideline earners—the Rolling Stones. Within days, Bill was on stage with the band at the Red Lion pub in Sutton, Surrey. While his colleagues whipped up a storm with their enthusiasm and boyish looks, Bill's stone-faced expression and static stage presence provided a marked contrast. But somehow it worked.

charlie watts

THE STONE WHOSE FACE EXUDES a Buster Keaton-like pathos, Charles Robert Watts was born on June 2, 1941 in Islington, north London, the son of truck driver. After his family moved to Wembley in 1948, Charlie attended the Tylers Croft Secondary Modern School where he displayed an enthusiasm for art, soccer, and cricket. At 14, he acquired his first musical instrument, a banjo, although as a persistent tapper, he soon took it apart and reconstructed it as a rudimentary drum kit. After the real thing arrived at Christmas 1955, Charlie taught himself how to play by jamming along to jazz records.

He left school in 1957, studied design at Harrow Art School for three years, and graduated in 1960 to pursue a promising career in advertising. Already acutely fashion-conscious, Charlie was also an authority on jazz, particularly be-bop legend Charlie Parker, whom he celebrated in book form in 1961. (This small illustrated title, *Ode to a High-Flying Bird*, was published in 1964.) For a couple of years, Watts was in advertising by day, and part of Blues By Six, and then the fast-emerging Alexis Korner's Blues Incorporated, by night. But toward the end of 1962, Charlie tired of the balancing act and decided to give up the band.

Meanwhile, the Rolling Stones, who'd formed that summer, were having little luck with drummers. Mick Avory (who later joined the Kinks) didn't last long, and the group settled on Tony Chapman, who played alongside Bill Wyman in the Cliftons. In January 1963, Chapman was unceremoniously sacked and the Stones approached Watts, whom they'd long coveted, to fill the vacancy. Because his instinct told him that R&B was about to break big, he agreed. On January 14, 1963, Mick Jagger, Keith Richard, Brian Jones, Bill Wyman, and Charlie Watts, together with pianist Ian Stewart, played together for the first time at the Flamingo Club in Soho. The Stones were indubitably rolling.

chronology

1963

June 7 Single release: "Come On"/"I Want To Be Loved."

July 7 The group make their television debut miming to "Come On" on *Lucky Stars Summer Spin*.

September 10 After a chance meeting with Andrew Oldham, John Lennon, and Paul McCartney volunteer a new song, "I Wanna Be Your Man," as the Stones second single.

September 15 The Stones open the Great Pop Prom at the Royal Albert Hall, London. The Beatles top the bill.

September 29 Opening night of the Stones' first British tour at the New Victoria Theatre, London.

October 3 Keith gives Brian a black eye backstage before a show at the Odeon, Southend. The argument was over a chicken meal.

November 1 Single release: "I Wanna Be Your Man"/"Stoned."

December 20 The group are voted sixth British Vocal Group and fifth British Small Group in the *New Musical Express* readers' poll.

1964

January 1 The Stones' advert for Kellogg's Rice Krispies breakfast cereal is premiered on TV. That same evening, they perform "I Wanna Be Your Man" on the first edition of BBC-TV's new pop show, *Top of the Pops*.

January 7 Their second British tour kicks off at the Adelphi, Slough.

February 8 Another package tour gets underway at the Regal Theatre, Edmonton.

February 21 Single release: "Not Fade Away"/"Little By Little."

March 19 The group record a historic stereo

broadcast for BBC Radio at the Camden Theatre in London.

March 27 The Stones attend a party for one of Andrew Oldham's new discoveries, Adrienne Posta, where they are introduced to 17-year-old Marianne Faithfull.

April 8 The band are mobbed at the Mad Mod Ball, which takes place at the Empire Pool, Wembley.

April 17 LP release: *The Rolling Stones*.

April 19 The group fly to Switzerland for the annual Golden Rose television festival.

April 22 The President of the National Federation of Hairdressers speaks out against long hair, declaring that "The Rolling Stones are the worst. One of them looks as if he has got a feather duster on his head."

April 26 The band make a good impression at the *New Musical Express* Poll Winners' Concert at the Empire Pool, Wembley.

May 31 At the Empire Pool, Wembley, once more, this time for the Pop Hit Parade show.

June 1 The Stones fly to New York for their first visit to the U.S. Five hundred fans beseige the airport to greet them.

June 3 The group are insulted by host Dean Martin after recording a spot for the *Hollywood Palace* television show.

June 10–11 A historic moment: The group spend two days recording at Chess Studios, Chicago, the spiritual home of R&B.

June 22 The Stones fly home to fulfil a booking they'd made months earlier, at the Commemoration Ball, at Magdalen College, Oxford.

June 26 Single release: "It's All Over Now"/ "Good Times, Bad Times." The Stones make a hastily arranged homecoming appearance on the pop show *Ready, Steady, Go!* Later that evening, they play at the All Night Rave at the Alexandra Palace, London.

July 4 The group make disparaging remarks about the week's record releases on the BBC-TV pop show *Juke Box Jury*.

July 24 Fans riot at the Stones' show at the Empress Ballroom, Blackpool.

August 2 The Stones headline an open-air festival at Longleat House in Wiltshire, the stately home of the Marquess of Bath.

August 7 Another bill-topping date, this time at the fourth National Jazz & Blues Festival in Richmond, Surrey.

September 5 The Stones embark on another U.K. tour, opening at the Finsbury Park Astoria, London.

September 11 "Laurie Yarham" wins a Mick Jagger lookalike competition—then declares he is Mick's brother, Chris.

October 14 Charlie Watts marries Shirley Ann Shepherd in secret at Bradford Registry Office.

October 23 The Stones fly to the United States for a three-week tour.

October 28 The group film five songs for an all-star concert film, *The TAMI Show*, in Santa Monica, California.

November 13 Single release: "Little Red Rooster"/"Off The Hook."

November 26 Mick Jagger is fined £16 for traffic offenses.

1965

January 6 A tour of Ireland begins with two shows at the ABC Theatre in Belfast.

January 15 LP release: *The Rolling Stones No. 2*.

January 21 The Stones arrive in Sydney for a month-long tour of Australia and New Zealand.

February 26 Single release: "The Last Time"/"Play With Fire."

March 5 A two-week British tour begins with two shows at the Regal, Edmonton.

March 24 The Stones arrive in Copenhagen for a tour of Scandinavia.

April 11 The band appear at the *New Musical Express* Poll Winners' Concert, which takes place at the Empire Pool, Wembley. They head the Best New Group and Best R&B Group categories.

April 23 A concert in Montreal, Canada, kicks off the Stones' third tour of North America.

July 10 The Stones triumph over the Beatles in the popularity stakes of Radio Luxembourg's Battle of the Giants competition.

July 22 Mick, Brian, and Bill are fined £5 each for

insulting behavior after urinating against a garage wall in Romford, Essex.

August 20 Single release: "(I Can't Get No) Satisfaction"/"The Spider And The Fly."

September 3 The Stones fly out to Dublin, accompanied by movie-maker Peter Whitehead, for a two-day tour of Ireland.

September 24 LP release: *Out Of Our Heads*. The group begin another British tour with two shows at the Finsbury Park Astoria.

October 22 Single release: "Get Off Of My Cloud"/"The Singer Not The Song."

October 27 The band arrive in New York for a six-week tour of the United States.

1966

February 4 Single release: "19th Nervous Breakdown"/"As Tears Go By."

February 16 The Stones arrive in Sydney for a two-week tour of Australasia.

April 15 LP release: *Aftermath*.

May 1 The Stones return to the Empire Pool, Wembley, for their third consecutive appearance at the *NME* Poll Winners' Concert.

May 13 Single release: "Paint It Black"/"Long Long While."

June 23 The Stones touch down in New York for another U.S. tour.

September 10 Peter Whitehead shoots footage of the group dressed in drag for use in a promotional film for their forthcoming single.

September 23 Single release: "Have You Seen Your Mother, Baby, Standing In The Shadow?"/ "Who's Driving Your Plane." The Rolling Stones' 1966 British tour begins with a show at the Royal Albert Hall, London.

October 15 Mick Jagger and Marianne Faithfull appear together publicly for the first time at a London launch party for underground magazine *International Times*.

December 19 Mick Jagger and Chrissie Shrimpton announce that their relationship is over.

1967

January 13 Single release: "Let's Spend The Night Together"/"Ruby Tuesday."

January 20 LP release: *Between The Buttons*.

January 22 The Stones refuse to participate in the all-star finale on *Sunday Night at the London Palladium* TV show.

February 5 The *News of the World* claims Mick Jagger took LSD at a pop star party. On the *Eamonn Andrews Show* later that day, Jagger announces he will be suing the paper.

February 12 Police raid Keith Richard's Redlands home and take various substances away for analysis.

February 19 The *News of the World* runs an exclusive report under the headline "Drugs Squad Raid Pop Stars Party."

February 25 Mick, Keith, and Brian leave the country and head for Morocco.

March 24 The group fly to Sweden to begin a European tour.

May 10 Mick, Keith, and Robert Fraser face drug charges in Chichester; each is released on £100 bail. Back in London, Brian Jones is arrested and charged with possession of drugs.

June 8 Brian drops in at a Beatles recording session at Abbey Road. He plays sax on "You Know My Name (Look Up The Number)."

June 18 Brian introduces the Jimi Hendrix Experience to an eager American public from the stage of the Monterey Pop Festival in California.

June 25 Mick, Keith, and Marianne join the Beatles for the live satellite television broadcast of "All You Need is Love."

June 27 Mick Jagger is found guilty of drug charges arising from the Redlands bust.

June 28 Brian Jones is busted at home.

June 29 Keith Richard is found guilty of drug charges and sentenced to one year in jail.

June 30 Mick and Keith are both released on bail.

July 31 Mick and Keith successfully appeal against their convictions.

August 18 Single release: "We Love You"/ "Dandelion."

August 25 Mick and Marianne travel to Bangor, in Wales, to join the Maharishi's weekend seminar on Transcendental Meditation.

September 29 It is announced that the group have parted with their manager, Andrew Oldham.

October 30 Brian Jones is sentenced to nine months in jail on drug charges.

December 8 LP release: *Their Satanic Majesties Request*.

December 12 Jones' jail sentence is quashed and he is fined £1,000 instead.

December 20 In the *New Musical Express*'s annual poll, the band come in at No. 4 in the World Vocal Group category. Mick was ranked 16th World's Male Singer.

1968

March 17 Mick Jagger attends a demonstration outside the American Embassy in Grosvenor Square, London, to protest against U.S. involvement in the Vietnam war.

May 7 It is announced Mick is to make his acting debut in a Warner Brothers movie, *The Performers* (later retitled *Performance*).

May 12 The group appear again at the *New Musical Express* Poll Winners' Concert at the Empire Pool, Wembley.

May 21 Brian Jones is charged with possession of cannabis after a raid at his home.

May 25 Single release: "Jumpin' Jack Flash"/"Child Of The Moon."

September 26 Brian is found guilty of drug charges and narrowly avoids a jail sentence.

October 12 Mick Jagger debates marriage and morality on television with "clean-up TV" campaigner Mary Whitehouse.

November 20 It is announced Marianne Faithfull has miscarried, losing Mick's baby.

December 5 LP release: *Beggars Banquet*. The Stones throw a launch party (and some pies).

December 10–12 The band films the *Rolling Stones' Rock 'n' Roll Circus*.

1969

May 28 Mick and Marianne are arrested at their London home. They are later charged with possessing cannabis.

May 30 Mick Taylor sits in on his first Rolling Stones recording session.

June 8 It is announced Brian Jones has left the Rolling Stones.

June 13 Mick Taylor is presented to the world's press at a photo call in London's Hyde Park.

July 2 Shortly before midnight, Brian Jones is found unconscious in his swimming pool at Cotchford Farm, Sussex.

July 4 Single release: "Honky Tonk Women"/ "You Can't Always Get What You Want."

July 5 The Stones headline a free concert in London's Hyde Park. It is billed as a tribute to Brian Jones.

July 8 Mick, accompanied by Marianne Faithfull, jets in to Sydney, Australia, to start filming *Ned Kelly*. After overdosing in a Sydney hotel, Marianne slips into a coma.

July 9 The coroner declares that Brian Jones' death was caused by "misadventure."

July 10 Brian is buried in Cheltenham.

August 10 Marlon, son of Keith Richard and Anita Pallenberg, is born.

November 7 The Stones begin their first American tour since 1966.

December 5 LP release: *Let It Bleed*.

December 6 The free show at the Altamont Speedway, California, ends in tragedy when one youth is stabbed to death in front of the stage while the group are playing.

December 14 The Stones play two homecoming shows at the Saville Theatre, London.

December 21 The group stage two additional London shows, this time at the Lyceum.

1970

June 24 *Ned Kelly* premieres in London. Mick Jagger does not attend.

July 29 The Stones announce they have severed their ties with American Allen Klein and his company, ABKCO.

July 31 The band's lengthy association with Decca Records ends.

September 2 The Stones embark on another European tour with a concert at the Olympic Stadium in Helsinki, Finland.

September 6 LP release: *Get Yer Ya-Ya's Out!*

October 12 Mick flies into London accompanied by a mysterious new girlfriend, Bianca Pérez Moreno de Macías.

November 7 The first Mick Jagger solo single, "Memo From Turner," featured in the movie *Performance*, is released.

December 5 *Gimme Shelter*, the documentary movie of the Stones' 1969 American tour, receives its premiere in New York.

1971

February 6 The Stones declare they will be moving to France as tax exiles and announce a farewell tour of Britain.

March 4 The tour begins with a show at the Newcastle City Hall.

March 14 The tour ends with two shows at the Roundhouse, London.

April 6 The Stones sign a deal with the Kinney Group. Their own Rolling Stones Records label will be distributed by Atlantic.

April 16 Single release: "Brown Sugar"/"Bitch"/ "Let It Rock."

April 23 LP release: *Sticky Fingers*.

May 12 Mick and Bianca marry at a ceremony in St.-Tropez in the south of France.

October 8 *Brian Jones Presents The Pipes Of Pan At Joujouka* is released on Rolling Stones Records.

October 21 Bianca Jagger gives birth to a daughter, Jade.

1972

April 14 Single release: "Tumbling Dice"/"Sweet Black Angel."

April 17 Anita Pallenberg gives birth to a second child, daughter Dandelion.

May 26 LP release: *Exile On Main Street*.

June 3 The Stones begin another North American tour with a show in Vancouver, Canada.

July 26 The tour ends with a concert at Madison Square Garden, New York. The aftershow party also celebrates Mick Jagger's 29th birthday.

December 26 Mick and Bianca leave London for Nicaragua after an earthquake devastates the capital city, Managua.

1973

January 18 The Stones play a benefit show for victims of the Nicaraguan earthquake. It takes place at the Los Angeles Forum.

January 21 The band's Australasian tour begins with a show in Honolulu.

June 18 Marsha Hunt claims in court that Mick Jagger is the father of her daughter, Karis.

June 26 Keith and Anita are arrested in their London home. They are later charged with possessing drugs and firearms.

July 31 A fire destroys much of Redlands, Keith and Anita's Sussex home.

August 20 Single release: "Angie"/"Silver Train."

August 31 LP release: *Goats Head Soup*.

September 1 The Stones' European tour begins with a concert in Vienna, Austria.

September 6 The band hold a homecoming party at Blenheim Palace, Oxfordshire, the home of the Duke of Marlborough.

October 24 Keith Richard is fined £205 for illegal possession of drugs and firearms.

1974

May 10 Bill Wyman's *Monkey Grip* is released on Rolling Stones Records. It is the first solo album by a band member.

July 13 Keith Richard joins Ronnie Wood on stage in London for the first of two solo shows by the Faces' guitarist. He enjoys it so much he comes back for the second night.

July 26 Single release: "It's Only Rock 'n' Roll (But I Like It)"/"Through The Lonely Nights."

October 18 LP release: *It's Only Rock 'n' Roll*.

bibliography

Bonanno, Massimo. *The Rolling Stones Chronicle* (Plexus, 1990)

Carr, Roy. *The Rolling Stones: An Illustrated Record* (New English Library, 1976)

Dalton, David. *The Rolling Stones: The First Twenty Years* (Thames & Hudson, 1981)

Miles. *The Rolling Stones: A Visual Documentary* (Omnibus Press, 1994)

Rawlings, Terry & Badman, Keith, with Neil, Andrew. *Good Times Bad Times: The Definitive Diary of the Rolling Stones 1960–1969* (Complete Music, 1997)

Sandford, Christopher. *Mick Jagger* (Gollancz, 1993)

Wyman, Bill, with Coleman, Ray. *Stone Alone* (Viking, 1990)

Newspapers and magazines:
Billboard, Daily Express, Daily Herald, Daily Mail, Daily Mirror, Daily Sketch, Daily Telegraph, Disc, International Times, Los Angeles Free Press, Melody Maker, New Musical Express, News of the World, The People, Sunday Express, Sunday Mirror, Vogue

acknowledgments

This book is dedicated to Erika Lewis.

Special thanks to Julie-Anne Fraser for the shared enthusiasm and to Fiona Bleach for the sweets. Also to Karen Langley for "the Cheltenham days."

This book would not have been possible without Andy "Beatles" Davis, who introduced me to the project; Will Steeds, who commissioned it; Hugh Gallacher, who patiently dug out the photographs; and the dynamic duo of Suzanne Evins and Justina Leitão, who expertly steered the book through to completion.

A tip of the hat to Tony Ward at Watford; Nick Kent for Bookman Projects; the photographers: Peter Stone, Kent Gavin, Doreen Spooner, and Vic Crawshaw; the staff of the Mirror library at Canary Wharf; and to Chris Jagger for making several additional comments beyond the call of duty.